Cash In on Cash Flow

50 Tough-as-Nails Ideas for Revitalizing Your Business

A. David Silver

amacom

American Management Association

New York • Atlanta • Boston • Chicago • Kansas City • San Francisco • Washington, D.C.
Brussels • Toronto • Mexico City • Tokyo

This book is available at a special
discount when ordered in bulk quantities.
For information, contact Special Sales Department,
AMACOM, a division of American Managment Association,
135 West 50th Street, New York, NY 10020.

Library of Congress Cataloging-in-Publication Data

Silver, A. David (Aaron David), 1941–
    Cash in on cash flow : 50 tough-as-nails ideas for revitalizing your business / A. David Silver.
        p.   cm.
    Includes bibliographical references and index.
    ISBN 0-8144-0210-0
    1. Cost control.   2. Business enterprises—Finance.   I. Title.
HD47.3.S54   1994
658.15—dc20   93-29959
                                                          CIP

Printing number

10   9   8   7   6   5   4   3   2   1

To **Don H. Pace,** who has demonstrated ineluctably and most elegantly with Pace American Group, Inc., that successful entrepreneurship can occur for the over-fifty crowd as well as for the boomers

Contents

Introduction

Here's an offer I'll bet nobody has made you today:

> Buy this book for $24.95 and read it; then implement 25 to 50 of the strategies that are suggested herein, and your company's cash flow will triple in 90 days and triple again within the year.

"Yes, and elephants can fly," you say. Okay, you're not persuaded. Then read the introduction quickly and then make up your mind.

Is This a Description of You?

Would you say that your company's sales are flat? Are expenses rising and accounts payable stretching out? Are your competitors making a meal out of your former market share? Is it not as much fun to go to work as it used to be? Would you say that your company seems ineluctably stuck in quotidian mediocrity? Are you thinking about selling or raising capital but finding that your bottom line is too pathetic to get your price? Do you avoid your banker? Do you find yourself constantly blaming the economy for your company's sluggish performance? Have some key employees left to go elsewhere? Is anything going as *right* as you would like?

If the answer to any of these questions is yes, let me tell you right up front that *the problems aren't fatal*. You are not in a crisis, you are merely everyone's "stuffee." It is time to do unto others what they have been doing unto you: *Gatekeep.*

Gatekeeping is leveraging most of the companies and entities with which your company conducts business. If you are paying out more than you're bringing in or if you are paying for goods and services up front and then waiting months to get paid by your customers, you are being *inversely leveraged*, or, in the vernacular, stuffed. Who's stuffing you? Anyone in the operating expenses section of your income statement whose annual payment is increasing from year to year. Obviously, I don't know your company, but the following service providers are probably sticking it to you at their toll booths: your landlord, the telephone company, your insurance carriers (health, accident, property and casualty, and workers' compensation), your lawyers, your accountants, your lender, your advertising agency, the airlines and hotels you use for business trips, suppliers of components used to produce your product or deliver your service, and your employees.

No wonder you are getting tired of dragging yourself into work lately. You're being taken advantage of. But it's going to stop. This book is going to put the tools in your hand that will enable you to neutralize the tollgates of others and to erect your own. You are going to go on a journey with me, and at the end you'll be able to say to all these service providers the business equivalent of:

> If you don't do it my way, I will come over to your house and shoot your dog.

And believe me, they will begin to do things your way.

The Purpose of This Book: Stuffee Therapy

Think of me as your therapist. Come into my office, sit down in a comfortable chair. Spend a few hours with me, and I guarantee that you will leave here with at least 50 of the most innovative and tough-as-nails ideas of your career.

I'll give you a couple of tips for free while you're still wondering if you should buy this book. One is Silver's Rule of Body Reduction, which says that you can chip off 15% of anything and it will function just as well. This rule applies to expenses, but some careful planning is required to implement it well. We review the fundamentals of corporate liposuction in Stage One of the book.

Then there is Silver's Rule of 30s, which goes as follows: Even though your new product may be 30% more efficient and 30% faster than the competition's, it must also be 30% cheaper to capture at least a 30% market share. A gatekeeper *always* enters the market with the lowest priced product or service because that lines the customers up, and, as they line up, a highway is formed. As the customers line up to buy your product, they form a row of selling sites. Because you built the highway and own the tollgate, you can charge other vendors who seek to gain access to and sell to the customers that are lined up on your highway. In charging tolls to other vendors, you create multiple marketing channels using the customers' capital. Tell me that this is not a fun thing to do at the office, and I will send you to another shrink.

Cash In on Cash Flow is not a feel-good book of verbal fixatives and one-line palliatives to help you turn your company around. Some business writers assign spiritual values to the text of money—"Look within yourself. There's an inner force; pull it out. Then give yourself a standing O." Those kinds of business books do exactly the same amount of good for managing one's business efficiently that burying a black cat in a graveyard at midnight does for warts. Cheerleading is *not* the subject of this book. My message is simply this:

> If you read this book and implement its strategies, you will triple your company's cash flow in 90 days, then triple it again within the year.

Gatekeeping: Controlling Access to Assets

You are about to make an attitude adjustment in your management style. You are going to convert from being a manager whose company is constantly leveraged to being someone who consistently leverages just about everyone you deal with in business. No more Mr. Nice Guy. You'll be called Carvin' Marvin or Death March Larry after you implement the gatekeeping strategies in this book. I call this new management method *gatekeeping* because, like a tollgate, gatekeeping enables the company that controls access to its valuable assets to charge tolls in a variety of directions. The next time you pay a toll—an up-front fee that limits your access to something you want—think of changing every facet of your company so that it becomes a collector of up-front payments, rather than an up-front payer. In the simplest sense, that is what this book is about.

However, before diving head first into the pool, let's pause for a message from the Middle Ages. To persuade you of the seriousness of my message, I must first anchor it in history. The concept of wealth in Western civilization derives from a time 900 years ago when a small group of men for the first time achieved military advantage over a large group of men with approximately 8 inches of steel known as a *stirrup*.

   The stirrup significantly modified social organization in the early Middle Ages. It enabled men to wear armor while riding horses. Men who could afford armor became formidable tanks and could subdue men who fought on foot. The small farmer who could not afford armor became either a serf or a craftsman who made armor in the employ of the lord who captured his land. It was the stirrup that enabled men who wore armor in battles to leverage inversely every person they fought, captured land from, or conscripted into their service. The result of the invention of the stirrup was a change in the landholding pattern and the control of wealth for centuries to come.

   To carry that thought forward 900 years to today, any business entity—agency, supplier, customer, counsel, service provider, competitor, lender, landlord, investor—that causes you to make an up-front payment before providing you with whatever you want or need is metaphorically battling you, fully armored, from atop a horse while you throw pebbles at it from the ground. You are being inversely leveraged. What you want is to be atop the horse, fully armored, and to stuff your competition, vendors, lenders, customers, and agents.

   In the late 1960s the microchip created another significant change in our social organization. With instant access to information and a concomitant reduction of time and space in the pattern of events, large corporations that were so successful in developing assembly-line patterns of work in the nineteenth and twentieth centuries were unable to react as quickly to data as could entrepreneur- and raider-driven companies that gathered and implemented information. Entrepreneurship thrived from 1968—the year of the birth of the semi-conductor—and it still is one of the most potent forces in the world economy. Raiders are takeover entrepreneurs who understand financial leverage or who lack novel ideas but who have the desire for ownership and the courage to go after it.

   Rank the leaders in any industry in the United States, western Europe, Israel, or Japan according to market value (i.e., wealth created for founders and stockholders), and near the top of the list will be an entrepreneurial company—one either created since 1968 or taken over and streamlined by corporate raiders. We all know the names: Microsoft, Wal-Mart, Safeway, Sony, Turner Broadcasting, Conseco, Clayton Homes, Humana, Genentech, MCI, Policy Management Systems, McCaw Cellular, RJR Nabisco. The market value of Microsoft surpassed that of IBM in January 1993. And what distinguishes these companies is that they operate tollgates and charge others for the privilege of dealing with them. They are gatekeepers. Their unspoken common denominator is the rapid collection and use of information in an opportunistic—some say atavistic—manner that leverages others and enhances the gatekeepers' cash flow return on stockholders equity.*

Once you have learned the fundamentals of gatekeeping, you will never return to a conventional management style, whatever that may be.

The Four Steps to Tripling Your Cash Flow

Here's a summary of the steps we discuss in this book that will dramatically increase your company's cash flow.

1. *Raise cash quickly.* Just as you would do on a personal wellness program, so you must do on a company wellness program. Go on a diet—not on your body, but on your company's overhead.

We're going to slash costs in ten expense categories in order to create genuine liquidity—a pile of cash. And with the money we save, we will implement some unique gatekeeping strategies.

Here are the ten expense categories that usually creep up steadily over the years:

1. Rent
2. Communications
3. Employee health insurance
4. Legal fees
5. Advertising
6. Loan costs
7. Accounting
8. Travel
9. Raw materials
10. Employee costs

Slashing expenses is cathartic. After you have done it, you will be pumped up like a freshman wide receiver in his first bowl game: "Get me the ball. Get me the ball. I'm wide open."

2. *Determine what is core and what is peripheral.* The next ball you're going to run with takes more clarity of thought and better planning than does simply slashing costs with the zest of Conan the Barbarian. You move into Stage Two lean and mean, but move carefully, because

---

*At this writing, the Federal Trade Commission has begun investigating Microsoft for monopolistic practices. What tribute! Simultaneous with the announcement of this honor being paid Microsoft, the largest U.S. air carriers reported yet another year of operating losses and once more beseeched their government for protection. What an embarrassment!

you are going to sever some limbs from the company's tree. Stage Two deals with spinning off your company's peripheral assets and focusing your energies on its remaining core business. This exercise raises even more cash than does expense slashing.

To do spin-offs correctly, you must distinguish what is *core* from what is *peripheral*. It isn't always easy to make the distinction. For instance, a subsidiary that was acquired five years ago may be generating ample cash flow to justify your original investment. But the subsidiary takes up your time, requires personnel and space in your data-processing department, and adds to your accounting, legal, communications, and travel costs. Furthermore, sales are beginning to level off, and the subsidiary's market may be reaching a saturation point. On the other hand, it can be sold for five or six times its cash flow; in spinning it off, you can also reduce some overhead costs.

That seems fairly basic, doesn't it? But what might not be so basic is *how* you spin off a subsidiary or division. I want to persuade you to hold on to a piece of the action of every subsidiary, division, or department that you sell, dispose of, or spin off. That little piece, 15% or so, may produce a significant capital gain in the future with minimal effort on your part. This rule of thumb is known as Silver's Rule of the Tip. Nobody will miss the 15% tips you accumulate, but someday the tips may generate huge capital gains for you.

These spun-off subsidiaries, departments, and divisions may well perform spectacularly better if they are owned by their management teams, and your minority interest may become worth hundreds of millions of dollars. The Seibels Bruce Group, a Columbia, South Carolina, insurance holding company with a $45 million market value, spun off its data processing division, Policy Management Systems, which today has a market value of $1.2 billion. But Seibels Bruce did not hold on to enough long enough. By retaining a piece of the action, you can actually sell an asset twice. A coup of this proportion, if made repeatedly, can certainly make work seem like drop-kicking liabilities through the goalposts of pain.

3. *Revitalize your marketing strategies.* At this point you are sitting on some serious cash, and your company's cash flow has tripled or better. We enter Stage Three having created genuine liquidity and an enthusiasm for building the core business. Our goal remains to *multiply cash flow threefold in nine months.* To accomplish this we reexamine the three major aspects of any business: *finding, grinding,* and *minding.*

If you think marketing is finding customers, you are wrong. It is finding noncustomers. If you are reaching them through only one or two marketing channels, that is not nearly enough. You want to sell through dozens of channels, particularly those where the customer pays up-front. Think like a gatekeeper: Go for multiple tollgates, on multiple highways, that generate tolls in your coin boxes 24 hours a day while requiring very few people to staff them. In the words of legendary movie director Cecil B. deMille: "What do you mean he had 12 disciples? Give him thousands."

Four new and inexpensive marketing concepts are beginning to weave their way into the fabric of U.S. business. These concepts are ministirrups because each one leverages somebody, causing the person to pay your company or to give your company something for free. The four concepts are:

1. Locating noncustomers inexpensively
2. Using affinity marketing
3. Obtaining air space marketing
4. Cooperating with competitors

We explore these concepts in detail in Stage Three because they have cash-flow generating power and require no or nominal investment.

4. *Introduce only successful new products.* I have saved the best—Stage Four, new product innovation—for last. With a slimmed-down, back-to-basics, cash-rich company, you are in a position to introduce some highly effective, absolutely right-on products or services. If you do it right, and if you innovate the best new products or services, your competitors will fold their tents and leave for a less competitive arena. I am going to try to persuade you to compete with yourself before someone else does. The logic is this: If a product or service is worth something, it is worth replicating. Someone is going to "knock off" or imitate your winning products. Why not let that someone be you? If you want to maintain market share, invent a new category, at different price points, of your company's winning products or services and begin marketing it immediately. This protects you from outside competition.

But how do you know which new products or services to introduce? I can show you how to predict the success or failure of your new product before you spend the first dime on developing it. The formula spells out the cost of the new product or service innovation. We also discuss the process of bringing the innovation to market rapidly, effectively, and inexpensively.

Acquiring Tollgate Power

The concept of gatekeeping states that if your company does not and cannot extract tolls from others but instead pays them, then you are in the wrong business. Your first priority, after stockpiling some serious cash, is not to develop new marketing strategies but to acquire gatekeeper companies—companies that collect tolls from customers, noncustomers, suppliers, competitors, and service organizations. All of the great corporate raiders have acquired gatekeepers, and they have done it with either financial leverage or the takeover targets' internal leverage. The best gatekeepers to acquire are insurance companies, and most of the giants of raiderdom—Warren Buffett, Henry Singleton, Laurence Tisch, Saul Steinberg, and Harold Geneen, to name a few—who have created wealth without starting up innovative companies have done so, in part, by acquiring insurance companies.

Getting Your Heart Back

If you have fallen out of love with your company, you are working with your head and not your heart. A host of external forces has caused you to "eat your heart out." I want you to get your heart back and to go to work heart first.

Gatekeeper managers set up their jobs in a manner that maximizes their convenience. They live near their work, either a short drive or a long walk away. They wear whatever they like to work. They select coworkers who have similar values. They accept *all* of the responsibility for their decisions. They do not fear failure because the thing they are building is constantly changing and neither failure nor success is quantifiable when there are so many unknowns. They are free to choose their own destiny, and, although they know that failure would mean losing that freedom, they move too rapidly to think about failure.

People who have their hearts in their jobs always beat people who work solely with their minds. You rarely hear someone who owns a piece of the action say, "I don't have my heart in my job." When we are fighting for turf, our equity interest, we give it 24 hours if necessary. In the early days of CNN, his cable TV station, Ted Turner put a cot in his office and lived there until he solved the company's problems. For him, failure was not a possibility.

At the end of each chapter in Stage One, there is a scorecard that summarizes the dollar amount of cash that you have saved or generated by implementing the strategies described in that chapter. In the interests of establishing a baseline, I assume that you own or manage a $5 million (annual revenues) manufacturing company or a $20 million distribution or retailing company. (From time to time, I refer to a scorecard for a $10 million service company model.) Numbers of employees, operating ratios, and individual operating expense items are based on publicly available industry data. If your company is larger or smaller than the two models, you can make calculations in the spaces provided to derive exact numbers for your company.

The summary in Chapter 25 includes a checklist to guide you in the step-by-step process of becoming a gatekeeper manager. Remember what it was like to win in business? Remember the joy of inch-by-inch progress against a fierce competitor, the warm feeling of landing a big reorder, of having one of the industry's top salespersons call and say she would like to join your team? It's going to happen again. You will become the *stuffer*, not the *stuffee*, to borrow a phrase from basketball.

Fifteen months from now you will be running a company with so many marketing channels that your interest income on idle cash and short-term investments will exceed your present net operating income. That is a slam-dunk promise.

A Final Reminder

If businesspeople like what they read and act on some of my ideas for gatekeeper management, then life in some industries is going to resemble musical chairs, with companies scrambling to capture market share using gatekeeper methods. Industries are not stagnant. The only thing certain in business is that there will be change. And if you do not program yourself for change, your competitors will program you their way.

Prologue

The following is an example of the kinds of changes discussed in this book:

A-to-Z Graphics in Mt. Olive, Ohio, has revenue of $5 million per annum, derived primarily from the wholesale distribution of artists' materials to retail stores in the Midwest (Ohio, western Pennsylvania, eastern Kentucky, Indiana, southwestern New York, southeastern Michigan, and West Virginia). It has eight salespersons who make sales calls on the stores two or three days per week. There is no prospecting; artists' supply stores are the only customers, and they are all listed in telephone books. A-to-Z Graphics does not sell to end users.

Phil Zicarelli, the owner of A-to-Z, had borrowed $1.2 million to buy out his partner, Al, and had pledged all of the company's assets. The bank was demanding that the loan, which was down to $800,000 in April 1993, be paid in full. Phil called me in to see if I could refinance the loan with another lender.

I reviewed A-to-Z's balance sheet. Accounts receivable were more than $560,000 and turning every 27 days. Inventory (about $1.2 million) was all finished goods and reasonably fresh. The building was carried on the books at $400,000, and there were several vehicles worth a total of $40,000. Using conventional borrowing ratios, I figured I could borrow up to $1.38 million for A-to-Z, of which $1.08 million would be in the form of a revolving line of credit and $300,000 would be a five-year term loan. Interest would run about $120,000 per annum and debt service about $80,000 per annum.

All was well and good on the balance sheet, but there was no cash flow to service the debt. In fact, A-to-Z was losing money—about $125,000 last year—and that, of course, was why the loan had been called even though it was being paid down.

I had 30 days to turn the company back into the black and take the loan to another lender. Failing that, the bank would start to foreclose, and the business would be irreparably damaged; the industry lives on credit reports.

Here is what a gatekeeper would have done, and what I did. First, I analyzed all overhead expense items, but I could find barely a penny to save. The problem was with marketing, and it was twofold: (1) expenses for the sales team were way out of line, and (2) the market outside the Midwest was being totally ignored.

An A-to-Z Salesperson's Compensation

The company was paying its salespeople a base of $350 per week for the first 26 weeks, charged against commissions. The commission structure was 5% of sales. Furthermore, the company paid the salespeople's expenses of about $1,000 to $1,200 per month, gave them cars to use, and paid for their health insurance—about $218 per month. The benefits to the sales staff were as follows:

Benefits to an A-to-Z Salesperson Before Commissions	
Expense reimbursement	$1,100
Automobile lease payments	264
Health insurance	218
Total	$1,582

Of the six salespeople, the three best had sales of $80,000 per month, on average, and were earning $4,000 per month, bringing their total compensation to $66,984 per year, of which roughly $19,000 was gifted to them. Moreover, the company's gross profit margin (gpm) had slipped over the last three years, dropping from 34.0 percent in 1990 to 32.2% in 1991 and to 29.9% in 1992. At sales of $5 million per annum, every 1% of gpm is worth $50,000 in pretax income. If I could get the company's gross profit margin back up to 33.0 percent, I would generate about $150,000 in cash flow and erase the debt. This could not be done in the short term but had to be part of a long-term change in habits among the sales team.

The sales team was accounting for roughly 55% of sales, or $2.75 million. The balance of the orders were house accounts: hundreds of artists' supply stores in the Midwest that had one of the company's catalogs from several years ago. It took five people on the telephone to handle the incoming orders, whose average size was $75.00.

Three outside salesmen were doing just about all of the $2.75 million in selling; the other three couldn't cut the mustard but were each costing the company $1,582 per month, or $4,746 per month and $56,952 per annum for the three salesmen.

With the owner's approval, I sacked the three nonperforming salespersons and sold their cars to raise $12,000 in cash. I lined the other three up against a hypothetical wall and told them that henceforth their commissions would be 15% of gross profit margins up to sales of $1 million per year and 20% of gpm for sales above $1 million; I also told them that they should recruit, hire, and train salespersons to work under them, for which they would be given an override of 2.5 to 5% per year. No longer would their expenses be paid; they would have to buy the cars from the company, and their health insurance was going to change to catastrophic coverage only—they would have to pay for checkups, cuts, and bruises.

Their jaws dropped so low I could see their inlays. "Why pick on us?" they demanded to know.

"We are the straw that stirs the drink around here," they protested.

I told them that they were each free-riding at the rate of $1,600 per month in benefits and that the company was no longer going to carry them for that amount. If they were good salespeople, they could make it up in commissions. The commission to them for a $10,000 sale at a 33% gpm under the new scheme would be $500. If they let the gpm slip below 30%, there would be no commission. Under the old commission scheme, they had received $500 no matter what. If they could not generate another dollar's sales, they could hire and train three people, and if those three people each sold $50,000 per month of goods at a 33% gpm, the override would be $1,980 per month.

They still didn't get it. So I explained it in gatekeeper talk: *"If you don't agree to the new compensation plan and leave this room with a cheer for ol' Dave, I will come over to your house and shoot your dog."*

"Look," I said. "The company provides you with a product line of several thousand highly salable products. Right? It has invested in building its name and its franchise in the Midwest over several decades. Right? It finances the cost of acquiring the inventory and stocking it so that when you make a sale and phone it in, the goods are there to be shipped. The company also finances the customer for 30 to 45 days until it pays for the purchase. Is all of this accurate so far?"

They nodded.

"This is not a market in which you have to search for leads or hunt for prospects. You don't have to waste one single, little, itty-bitty moment searching for customers. Nor does the company interfere with your territory or fight you over inside versus outside sales. If you make the contact and the first sale, that customer is yours, even when it calls in orders. You are supported with advertising in the trade journals and trade show booths. Is this true?"

They nodded.

"Then you should get down on your hands and knees and thank the Lord that the company has made your bed, pulled down the spread, and put a piece of chocolate on the pillow, because you are really blessed. No capital outlay. Just your time."

They agreed. They agreed to stay, as well. We sold them their cars for $18,000 and brought another $4,800 to the bottom line.

How could I take such a hard line? How could I tollgate the three people who were accounting for 55 percent of sales? The logic was in my favor. The owner had mistaken his role. He thought he was in bondage to the salesforce.

But I had a telemarketing card up my sleeve, and I played it first.

A-to-Z had been concentrating all of its marketing energy in the upper Midwest, ignoring the rest of North America. Its competitors attempted to pick off A-to-Z's midwestern customers, but A-to-Z had never made a move on theirs. But, as Dr. Samuel Johnson so eloquently put it, a hanging focuses the mind.

I called the publisher of the artists' supplies retailers' leading trade journal, and we discussed his readership, the number of subscribers, and the quality of the list. He had 15,000 names, but his software could not weed out the midwestern names. I would have to buy the whole list at $50 per thousand, or $750, and weed out the midwestern names. Knowing a little bit about barter, I asked him if I could insert his subscription renewal cards in my mailing and rent his list for free. He agreed and mailed me the 15,000 names and addresses on Cheshire labels, along with 15,000 subscription renewal forms. These arrived in two days.

In the interim I called the local high schools and hired some envelope stuffers. I also called the nearest community college and hired the top software programmer to design and lay out a marketing piece to overlay the catalog that I intended to mail to A-to-Z's noncustomers in its nonmarkets.

My goal was to create a positive cash flow in the current month and then to sustain it throughout the year in order to service new debt and put the company on a firm financial footing. Because the direct-marketing strategy did not require the payment of commissions, the idea for the headline of the promotion was to guarantee a price significantly below the competition's and to hold it there. Because our gpm was 33% at full wholesale, after which we gave up another 15% (of sales) in the form of commissions, I could afford to make a 20% gpm on the sale and come in 13% below the best price my competitors could offer. Actually, I could offer a steeper discount—down to a gpm of 18%—but I wanted to offer free delivery to make a deep dent in these new markets. I figured a typical sale to earn the following:

		$	%
(a)	Average unit price (full whlsle)	$125.00	
(b)	Discounted price in direct marketing blitz (b) = (a) × .87 =	108.75	102.3%
(c)	Less UPS two-day delivery expense	2.50	2.3
	Total of (b) − (c)	$106.25	100.0%
(d)	Cost of goods sold	83.37	78.5
(e)	Gross profit margin	$ 22.88	21.5%

How many sales did I have to make in the first month to reverse the $10,000 monthly loss and to generate $20,000 in cash flow to demonstrate debt-service capability? The mailing piece, at 69 cents per envelope—discounted because we used a presorter service—would cost $6,900 for postage and another $1,500 in labor for weeding out the midwestern names and stuffing and labeling the envelopes. The inside salesperson could handle the incoming orders. I would offer 30-day terms. To limit the cost of bad debts, I would limit initial orders to $500.00. Still, I estimated that A-to-Z would get hit with $5,000, or 20 orders, worth of bad debts. Thus, my additional costs would be $13,400, which increased my target cash flow to $43,400. By dividing gpm of 21.5% into the hurdle of $43,400, I determined that I had to achieve sales of $201,860. Assuming an average ticket of $125.00 per sales, that meant 1,615 individual unit sales, or a 16.1% response on 10,000 mailings.

To make sure I achieved a high response rate, I developed a stronger-than-usual headline. It read as follows:

PRICES SLASHED TO THE BONE. MUST SELL OVERSTOCKED ITEMS IMMEDIATELY. WE GUARANTEE THAT OUR PRICES ARE BELOW THE COMPETITION'S. SEE OUR LIST. FAX US YOUR ORDER NOW. WE

WILL DELIVER IN TWO DAYS VIA UPS. YOU HAVE 30 DAYS TO PAY. OFFER GOOD TO END OF MONTH.

Conditions of Sale: Limit of $500 per first order. If you can produce an invoice from a vendor that indicates a price lower than that offered by A-to-Z, we will adjust our price to 10% below that invoice.

Following the headline and subheadline were A-to-Z's 800 number, fax number, and mailing address. These were followed by the catalog with old prices marked through and new ones at the discounted rates printed in.

We staggered the mailings to 1,000 per day over ten days so that we would not disappoint the new customers with busy signals when they called in.

One day before the mailing I decided to test the viability of the telemarketing concept. We had a time zone advantage in the Central, Mountain, and Pacific zones. I asked my inbound sales people to stay late and make 30 to 50 random calls each to artists' supply stores located west of us and to then fax catalog pages. I gave them each $30 plus dinner to stay late and promised a $200 bonus to the person who made the most sales and $100 to the second-place finisher.

We got on the telephones at 5:00 P.M. that night. Within three and a half hours, the seven of us had made 286 telephone calls in which we spoke to someone with ordering ability. We generated a response rate of 31 percent, or 89 sales. The sales averaged $162.50, resulting in $14,462.50 in new business and $3,109 in cash flow. The telephone calls and faxes cost:

330 connected calls at $1.50	$ 495.00
286 calls beyond 1 minute	189.00
286 faxes at $.085/page × 5 pages	122.00
Dinner plus overtime	245.00
Bonuses	300.00
Total cost	1,351.00
Net cash flow	$1,758.00

The inside calling team got pretty enthused about the program, and the next day they met and agreed to do it again. But they wanted to spread the $300 in bonus money a little more evenly: $150 to the evening's winner, $100 for second place, and $50 for third place. They also wanted me to bring a second fax into the "war room" to avoid the previous night's jam-up.

We operated the telemarketing strategy for the next 30 days and did the mailing simultaneously. One program supported the other in a symbiosis that was far greater than I had imagined. Our response rate leapt to 52.5%, and we gained 4,786 new customers (some of the addresses we had were incorrect, obsolete, or "return to sender"). After the fifth day, we stopped faxing because our mail solicitations had arrived, so we saved $3,050 in fax costs.

The telemarketing-plus-direct-mail program generated 4,786 new customers who ordered $154.85 on average, or $741,112, on which we made a gross profit of $159,339. The cost of the program was $12,400 (bad debts came to $4,000 rather than the predicted $5,000) for the direct-mail portion and $37,351 for the telemarketing portion, resulting in net cash flow before corporate overhead (or "contribution") of:

Gross profit	$159,339
Less: Direct Mail	12,400
Less: Telemarketing	37,351
Net contribution	$109,588

The program was more successful than projected, and A-to-Z's owner, Phil, accepted the challenge of the inside sales team, which bet that it could do even better in subsequent months. (Its members had been given some inside information by me that their jobs were in jeopardy if they didn't succeed at telemarketing, and people will raise their tollgates and get four-square behind an innovative idea in their department if you give them that kind of inside information.) Phil agreed to print new catalogs, and the inside/outside sales team wrote its own catchy and memorable headlines. It found another 2,224 customers out of the 9,500 names. Over the course of the next six months, the outside sales team, working three and a half hours per night, generated the following results, reported to me in this letter:

The inside sales team at A-to-Z Graphics reported the following sixth-month results:

Sales	$3,678,015
New Customers	7,010
Sales per New Customer per Month	$ 87.45

The inside sales team and I were able to flood A-to-Z Graphics with cash—over $650,000 in net cash flow in six months and $1.3 million in one year—by gaining the cooperation of disparate individuals and by bringing the outside sales team's marketing costs into line. The company was saved from becoming just another casualty of a frightened banker and an inversely leveraged owner. Did A-to-Z's competitors come into the Midwest with direct-mail programs and cut into its market share? They tried, but the company had put its midwestern customers into frequent purchaser clubs and the customers were too wedded to the company to desert it.

Stage One
Slashing Costs

1

Talking to Your Landlord

The U.S. real estate industry lacked adult supervision for years. Having tax incentives thrown to it like puppy treat, it attracted gobs of people—people whom you wouldn't trust to run water, much less money—to build tall buildings, fat warehouses, and sprawling residential developments. Through all of the 1970s and much of the 1980s, banks, savings and loans, and insurance companies tossed high-interest-rate money at real estate developers with reckless abandon, until the United States became significantly overbuilt, with enough commercial space to meet projected needs well into the twenty-first century.

To repay their lenders, owners of commercial real estate do what comes naturally—stick it to their tenants. If you haven't read your company's lease (or leases, if you have multiple locations) for a few years, you are in for a big surprise. You are about to receive a windfall. Here are some true stories from the early 1990s.

A Los Angeles Leverage

There are more than 600 tenants in the South Grand Avenue building in downtown Los Angeles, a building that houses the bulk of that city's garment manufacturers. The tenants of South Grand each received a 33% rent reduction in 1992 because they demanded that the building's owner roll back their rents or face mass defections. One of the tenants, a dress manufacturer, said he was bluffing, and he believes that many of the other tenants were, as well. But the landlord couldn't know this, and attracting new tenants in the depths of a recession was not the owner's idea of a good time. So the landlord blinked and reduced the rents for all of the tenants by 33%.

What does this mean? It means that in this particular building, in this particular city, in the recession of 1991–1992, the building's owner was *tollgated* by his tenants, which is an admission of the following facts: (1) Rents were too high to begin with, (2) the owner did not want to have empty spaces, and (3) when tenants cooperate to get their rents lowered, they generally succeed.

A New York Nullifier

At approximately the same time, the tenants of one of New York City's largest midtown office buildings stopped paying rent because they ran out of money and could not afford to pay it. Moreover, the tenants were for the most part law firms, law firms full of lawyers who had sworn oaths to act as trustees of their state's laws. Yet they were stiffing their landlord.

The building's owner hired counsel to begin evicting the tenants, and he did so with relish, floor by floor. He needed the work. But after about a dozen evictions, the owner called off his lawyer, saying, "Stop the evictions. I can't rent the empty offices with so many vacancies. It looks bad. The prospective tenants think something is wrong."

About a year went by, with the owner collecting nearly no rent and making no payments on its mortgage loan to one of New York City's major banks. With guilt and fear of foreclosure causing tremors and extremes of anxiety, the owner visited his banker to hand him the keys to the building.

"Here, take the building in full payment of the loan," said the owner to the banker.

"Why?" asked the banker.

"Because I can't collect rents, and I can't throw the tenants out. So I'm stuck."

To the owner's amazement, the banker threw the keys back at him, saying, "I don't want the building. If I take the building, the auditors will make me write the loan down to the building's true worth, which is probably half the value of the loan. It will be a charge against the bank's net worth. And I could lose my job for making such a bad loan."

"What should I do?" asked the owner.

"Pay me what you can, and let's hope the auditors don't question the loan. If they do, we'll write a new loan, with deferred principal payments and affordable interest."

Auditors are in business to make money, not to force their banks to write down loans. Thus, many of them do not dig into the portfolios of large commercial banks, savings and loans, and insurance companies, as anyone who has followed the savings and loan or

BCCI scandals of the early 1990s is painfully aware. Auditors want to hold on to as many clients in the financing industries as possible because financial institutions are sources of new leads for auditors.

"It's happening all over New York," I was told by a well-informed real estate attorney. The peculiar difference between the Los Angeles and the New York City stories is that the Los Angeles apparel manufacturers joined forces to obtain rent reductions, whereas the New York tenants acted independently, perhaps out of shame, and achieved free tenancy.

The RTC Factor

The rent equation may be made more complicated if your landlord's mortgage loan is held by a troubled lender that has been seized by the Resolution Trust Corporation (RTC). This government agency is empowered to foreclose on troubled banks, wrap up their operations, place a tourniquet on cash outflow, then sell off the underlying assets—including the building that you are renting space in—at auction. The buy-in prices at auction have been running at approximately 50% of appraised value. Some excellent buildings have been picked up at RTC auctions at unbelievably low prices.

RTC employees are not poster children for the local petting zoos. They are not warm and sensitive individuals. They have a job to do, and if people get hurt in the process, that's their tough luck. Accordingly, some landlords and some tenants in different parts of the country, acting independently of each other, have stopped making payments on their mortgages or paying their rents with the intent of catalyzing the downslide of the bank into the outstretched waiting arms of the RTC. The goal is to achieve a lower rent based on the building's new owner's bargain purchase. The tactic, however, devastates the building owner's net worth. It is high-stakes poker, extremely unethical, and absolutely not recommended for those who value social utility above personal wealth.

The Tenant as Gatekeeper

Let's look at these three stories "gatekeeperistically." Tenants in the 1990s have leverage over landlords, partly because the tenants know (information is the source of gatekeeper power), and landlords know they know, that landlords have been gouging their tenants for at least ten years, or from the date that junk bond and highly leveraged

transactions were invented. Rents rose to whatever level was necessary to make the landlords' highly leveraged real estate loans show a
positive cash flow. The tenants know they have been getting stuffed
for more than ten years.

Landlords have tollgate power over the banks who granted them
too much debt on too small an equity base so they could buy or build
their commercial buildings. As evidence of this, consider that some
landlords have successfully sued lenders for providing excessive
leverage that the lenders knew the landlords could not hope to repay,
thus wiping out the landlords' equity. But the principal reason that
landlords have leverage over their mortgage holders is that there are
billions of dollars of nonperforming real estate loans in the U.S.
economy that the accounting profession (a possible oxymoron in the
context of nonperforming loans) is not pushing its clients to write off.
If the accountants did clean up the books, many of the leading
commercial banks and insurance companies in America would file for
protection under Chapter 11, wiping out savings accounts, annuities,
life insurance claims, and investments of mutual funds and pension
funds and seriously altering life on the planet.

All of which means that you, the tenant, have more power than
you perhaps believed possible.

What does this mean? It means that a tenant is not alone in his
or her landlord relations. There are other economic players in this
new game. The tenant has a supporting cast—other tenants, a careful
reading of the lease agreement, and gatekeeper tactics—and the
building owner has a supporting cast—the banker, the bank's board
of directors and stockholders, the bank's auditors, and the RTC. In
the New York City story, the building's owner thought he was being
leveraged by the nonpaying tenants, only to learn that he had
leverage over his banker because the banker had leverage over the
bank's auditors, who were responsible to the bank's board of directors. In the Los Angeles story, by joining arms and demanding a rent
reduction, 600 tenants leveraged their landlord. That was a made-to-
happen slam dunk.

The RTC example describes an unethical, if not illegal, means of
forcing lower rents by destroying lenders. Note that without government intervention—the imposition of the RTC—the opportunity to
drive banks into the clutches of the RTC would not exist.

Are You All Alone When You're All Alone?

Ah, but you protest. Your company is the sole tenant in a building. It
lacks leverage. It has no other tenant with which to cooperate.

Don't think for a minute that you are all alone. Don't begin the process of tripling your cash flow in 90 days on a negative note.

Most building owners are stuffers, and most tenants are stuffees most of the time. You can reverse that condition even when you are all alone, because when you're a gatekeeper, you've got allies. *Information* is your best friend. Think for a minute. Where are the words that gave the landlord the power to stuff you? In the lease. The words are somewhere in the lease. Maybe there are words in the lease that can be interpreted in the tenant's favor. Let me explain.

How Many Square Feet?

Here the Rule of Body Reduction comes into play—in your favor, this time. Your landlord has been charging you for more space than actually exists. Pull out a copy of your lease and bring your tape measure from home. We are going to get back the 15% that the landlord inadvertently or otherwise began snipping out of your cash flow each year since you began renting from him.

The landlord more than likely took his measurements from a blueprint or from the outer walls. Remeasure the space from the inner walls; carefully go around the buttresses with your tape measure, excluding the electrical and telephone boxes. Then compare your total square footage number with the number in the lease. I would bet that your number is smaller. Here are two examples of what you are likely to find:

- Company ABC leases 5,780 square feet of office space at $19 per square foot per annum. An in-house measurement indicates a discrepancy of 867 square feet, or approximately 15%. Over a lease term of five years, the total recovery and/or savings could be over $70,000. If taxes and ancillary services such as janitorial services, security, insurance, utilities, and parking are taken into account, the overcharge claim could well increase to twice that amount.
- Company XYZ leases 30,500 square feet of warehouse space at $9.50 per square foot per year. An in-house measurement indicates a discrepancy of 3,050 square feet. Over a lease term of ten years, the total recovery and/or savings amounts to nearly $200,000 and possibly twice that amount when common-area factors are considered.

Are you beginning to see how much fun business can be when you begin collecting the money that others have been suctioning from you every year?

Common-Area Factors

Not only has your landlord miscalculated the actual space you are occupying, he is probably charging you for space you do not use at all. And you have been going along with it like a lamb for years. You are probably paying for "rentable" space—the "common areas" in the building—when you should be paying for "usable" space. Common areas include each tenant's pro rata share of the lobbies, corridors, restrooms, janitorial and electrical closets, and vending machine and other areas that are used or paid for by all tenants. If you are on an upper floor, your pro rate usage of the lobby is less than that of a first-floor tenant. Thus, your company should pay less for the common area. Is it paying less for the lobby? Read the lease.

Once you have discovered that you have been overcharged by your landlord, you will probably calculate two different dollar amounts: an amount correcting the miscalculation of the usable area occupied by your office and an amount correcting the overcharge you have been paying for the common area. It will require some skillful negotiating to capture the historical rent overcharges and to secure a rent adjustment going forward.

Before bursting into the landlord's office like Sheena, Queen of the Jaguars, study the lease carefully. Some landlords have gained experience in lease negotiations over the course of many battles and have inserted the word "approximate" into the lease before the words "rentable space." Of course, one person's "approximate" allows a 15% differential, and another person's, 1.5%. The word has different meanings for different people in different situations. The word "approximate" in the lease blunts your case, *except* if the term of the lease has been significantly long and the nominal $5,000 a year that you have been paying for rentable space adds up to $50,000 over ten years, plus lost interest. That is not an approximate number. That is a large number, as shown in Exhibit 1-1.

If your landlord has been putting his thumb on the scale for ten years and charging your company an extra $5,000 a year because his calculation of rentable space was off by some "approximate" percentage, then you are owed, fair and square, $55,304. Note the compounding effect of the money that the landlord has been "saving" for you. I selected an interest rate of 7.5% per annum to reflect an

Exhibit 1-1. Cost of 10 years' rent overpayments based on miscalculations of space.

Year	Overpayment	Interest @ 7.5% per annum	Amount due Tenant
1984	$5,000	$375	$ 5,375
1985	5,000	403	5,403
1986	5,000	433	5,433
1987	5,000	466	5,466
1988	5,000	501	5,501
1989	5,000	538	5,538
1990	5,000	579	5,579
1991	5,000	622	5,622
1992	5,000	668	5,668
1993	5,000	719	5,719
Total			$55,304

average of the high rates of the effluvial 1980s and the low rates of the more sanguine 1990s. You do not need an attorney to collect this money for you. Even if the landlord refuses to pay you, you still don't need an attorney, who'll take one-third of the $55,304 prize. You can do it all in-house with the help of the reference section of the nearest public library.

Recapturing the Common-Area Charges

In the local library, look for publications by the Building Owners and Managers Association (BOMA) and books, usually in the real estate or legal sections, that define technical lease terms, perhaps including those used in your state. BOMA, located in Chicago,* publishes guidelines for defining common-area factors and other terms, but I suspect their rules are toothless as a possible ally in your forthcoming battle. What you want to accomplish in round two of the negotiations is two things:

1. You want some money back, as well as a reduction in future rental payments, for space within or without the building that you do not use.

*The *Encyclopedia of Associations,* which is in the reference section of most public libraries, has the names, addresses, telephone numbers, and mission statements of hundreds of associations, including BOMA.

2. You want to be sure that, if your rent is net-net-net, you are not being charged on a full service basis.

Unused Space

Who uses lobbies? Do they have as much value to a tenth-floor tenant as they do to a tenant on the first floor? If I were on a high floor, I would be willing to pay a corridor width and length space from the front door to the elevator, but I would contest being charged a pro rata amount of the lobby space.

Let's assume that the entire lobby is 3,000 square feet and that there are ten tenants above the first floor and five retail tenants on the first floor. Each tenant has been paying one-fifteenth of 3,000 square feet as a common-area factor. But your visitors and customers do not use the retail shops in the lobby; thus, you believe that a fair common-area factor payment is one-tenth of the 300 square feet of corridor space from the door to the elevator only. The difference is $3,000 \times 6.6\% = 198$ square feet of common area per annum compared to $300 \times 10\% = 30$ square feet of common area per annum. If the building rents for $25.00 per square foot per year, then you have been overcharged by $4,200 per year. Over ten years, with interest compounding, you have just found a $40,0000 check in your lobby with your name on it.

Full Service vs. Net-Net-Net Leases

Before giving away the pro rata cost of the janitorial and electrical closets, examine your lease to determine if your company is receiving janitorial and electrical services as part of its lease.

A *full-service* lease includes all building services, maintenance, real estate taxes, janitorial services, and utilities. A *net-net-net* lease, on the other hand, usually indicates that the tenant pays separately for all taxes, utilities, insurance, and maintenance of the usable space and common areas.

If your lease is net-net-net, it is appropriate to demand some reduction in the common-area factor costs of the electrical and janitorial closets because some of the services that flow out of these closets are designated for items that you are not paying for, such as the parking lot, the entrance area, building signage, and basement storage.

If your company does not use the basement to store items or does not use its pro rata share of the parking lot, yet the janitor cleans these areas with equal vigor and energy and the building's electricity heats and lights these areas without prejudice, then you are being overcharged. The amount of the janitorial or electrical services overcharge could be about the same—168 square feet × $25.00 per square foot per year—as the common-area factor that you have been overcharged for lobby space that you do not use. Is the amount of money chickenfeed or chicken cordon bleu? The cost is calculated in Exhibit 1-2.

It is definitely an amount of money worth recapturing from your landlord.

Winning at Tollgate Negotiations

You have two amounts to collect from the landlord: the amount based on his miscalculation of the space your company actually rents and the amount based on common-area factor overcharges. In our example, the landlord owes you $55,304 for the former and $88,486 for the latter, plus a reduction of $5,000 per year for the former and $8,000 per year for the latter going foward. Your negotiating goal is to win all four points, and your leverage is impressive.

Exhibit 1-2. Cost of 10 years' rent overpayments based on common area factors.

Year	Lobby	Parking, Basement, Janitor's Closet, Electrical Closet	Interest @ 7.5% per annum	Amount due Tenant
1984	$4,200	$3,800	$ 600	$ 8,600
1985	4,200	3,800	656	8,645
1986	4,200	3,800	693	8,693
1987	4,200	3,800	745	8,745
1988	4,200	3,800	801	8,801
1989	4,200	3,800	861	8,861
1990	4,200	3,800	926	8,926
1991	4,200	3,800	995	8,995
1992	4,200	3,800	1,070	9,070
1993	4,200	3,800	1,150	9,150
Total				$88,486

Remember, if you do not get what you want, three outcomes are possible:

1. You can break the lease and go elsewhere, leaving the landlord with an empty space in a tough market.
2. You can organize a tenants' grievance association that could give the landlord a migraine headache ten times larger than a one-tenant problem.
3. If you have organized the tenants into a militant group, you can threaten to publicize your grievance in the local newspaper, which will certainly get an interesting response from the landlord as she awaits a telephone call from her banker or mortgage holder.

As you leave the landlord's office, point out these steps to her and give her five days to respond to your rollback request, after which you will go on to organize the other tenants.

Keep the Courtroom Out of Your Business

Let's say your landlord stonewalls the tenants' association. Do you sue? No. Why increase your legal costs? Why *invite* the courtroom to control your business? After all, when a business matter goes into court, there is no telling what a judge or jury may decide. (If a law firm is also a tenant and agrees to represent the association free of charge, then the litigation alternative is a possible arrow in your quiver.)

A more realistic alternative is for the tenants' association members to withhold from their monthly rental payments an amount equal to the monthly overcharge. Invest the aggregate monthly overcharges in a money market account. Inform the landlord that the overcharges are being paid into this account so that there is no misunderstanding about the tenants' ability to pay and so that the landlord cannot claim they are negotiating in bad faith.

If the landlord sues the tenants for underpayment, then the matter moves from a private to a public level. A business reporter for the local newspaper may find the story interesting. But before issuing a press release, draft one and send a copy to the landlord and ask for comment on its accuracy. Landlords want to profit in the commercial real estate business, and the last thing they want or need is a negative newspaper story. In all likelihood, you will hear that the lawsuit was filed in the "bad ideas folder," and in a few days you will be visited by a defanged landlord ready to negotiate.

When you have the facts on your side and when your opponent

can be hurt economically by the facts through bad publicity or by the desertion of his customers, you probably won't need a lawyer and the expense of litigation. In fact, if the landlord sues you or the tenants' association, you can be a more flexible opponent by representing yourself (action pro se, as it is referred to in legal circles).

It is only when you are wrong, or possibly wrong, that you need a lawyer. Otherwise, if you can read, you can represent yourself in most business dealings.

SCORECARD

Let's assume the $5 million (revenues) per annum manufacturing or service company rents 2,500 square feet of space and the $20 million (revenues) per annum distributor rents 15,000 square feet of space. The small company pays rent of $2.50 per square foot (psf) per month, or $30.00 psf per annum, or $75,000 total per year, and the midsize company pays rent of $3.75 per square foot per month, or $45.00 psf per annum, or $675,000 total per year. We further assume that both companies have been tenants in their current locations for five years and that the miscalculation of space overcharge has been 10% and the common-area factors overcharge has been 5%, for an aggregate overcharge for the small company of $75,000 × 15% or $11,250 per annum and an aggregate overcharge of $101,250 for the midsize company. By the way, there are income tax implications, financial statement restatements, and other consequences of gaining cash windfalls that you should discuss with your accountants. (Do not call them until you have read Chapter 7 on rolling back accounting and auditing costs.)

Box Score No. 1
Rent

Small Company

Year	Overpayment	Interest @ 7.5% per annum	Amount due tenant
1989	$11,250	$ 844	$12,094
1990	11,250	907	12,157
1991	11,250	975	12,225
1992	11,250	1,048	12,298
1993	11,250	1,127	12,377
Total			$61,151

Midsize Company

Year	Overpayment	Interest @ 7.5% per annum	Amount due tenant
1989	$101,250	$ 7,598	$108,844
1990	101,250	8,163	109,413
1991	101,250	8,776	110,026
1992	101,250	9,434	110,684
1993	101,250	10,141	111,391
Total			$550,358

How many hours will it take you to complete this negotiation? About 200, or one month's time, including the week or so that you allow the landlord to read the lease, consult with her lawyer, raise the money that she owes you, try to bluff you with the threat of five years of litigation, and finally capitulate. In 200 hours—one month— you have raised a beginning pile of cash of somewhere between $61,000 and $550,000 (based on our sample companies). Furthermore, your annual cash flow going forward has been improved by some- where between $12,000 and $108,000 per annum. Make a mental note that these are pretax adjustments; you will need to share some of your lucre with Uncle Sam.

2

Reexamining Your Communications Costs

While waiting for a response from your landlord to the issues raised in Chapter 1, you can begin finding buried treasure in your company's operating expenses. Communications costs harbor quite a bit of waste. I know of an insurance company that is so skilled at managing its communications costs that it makes a profit on telemarketing (dialing for dollars, in the vernacular). As I briefly explain how they do it, try to think associationally: "Do these strategies apply to anything that we do in my company? We are not in the insurance business, but we sell services via telemarketing and/or a sales force. Are there enough similarities to make copying these ideas feasible?"

Dialing for Dollars Profitably

The insurance company in question sells life and health insurance to small employee companies and groups. It has 1,000 selling agents in 48 states, and it rents prospect lists from the large list and directory publishers. The lists have the company's name, address, and telephone number and the name of the chief executive officer. The lists are rented twice a year and delivered to an insurance company subsidiary that employs telephone callers with pleasant voices.

The agents, who are independent contractors, pay the telemarketing company for leads at $10 per lead. The telemarketing subsidiary takes in the order—say, 20 small business owners in zip code 86301—and the telemarketers order a dump onto their hard disks of all the names in that and the surrounding zip codes. They begin calling.

Since most of the time that we spend on the telephone is spent dialing, waiting, finding that the party is not in, and giving a callback number, the telemarketing subsidiary uses a computer to do the dialing. The process is known as *predictive dialing.* The computer calls the numbers on the list; when it locates an owner who is in and brings him to the telephone, the CRT flashes in front of one of the telemarketing operators who is not busy. The operator can see:

James R. Jones
President
Meriwether & Clark Travel
1000 Stateway 22
Wilson, Wyoming 75728

The operator can then go right into the qualifying conversation, the goal of which is to ask, "May we send an agent to call on you?"

The concept of spinning off your sales force into independent contractors* or agents who pay your company for leads is a tantalizing idea with significant cash generating (or sales devastating) implications. We confront these issues in Stage Two.

Turning our attention to the telemarketing subsidiary, note that with the use of predictive dialing the insurance company generated six bona fide prospects per hour per telemarketing operator. Without predictive dialing, a typical telemarketing operator can generate only two prospects per hour. For a 60-person telemarketing team, that amounts to 360 prospects per day. The agents have the ability, on average, to close 30% of their leads, or 120 per day. With an average annual premium of $1,200, paid monthly, the insurance company increased its premiums to nearly $3 million per month from $1 million per month simply by installing predictive dialing. At a combined ratio of 88%, the company's profits increased to $360,000 per month from $120,000 per month. The predictive dialing system, which cost the insurance company $350,000 fully paid for and installed, was paid for in six weeks.

As the predictive dialing system went through the 8 million rented names—that is, called all 8 million telephone numbers on the list—it found and corrected about 15%, or 1.2 million names, thereby "cleaning the list" for its owner. When it sent the cleaned and updated list back to the owner, it charged the list owner three cents

---

*It is a repetitive theme of mine, and not solely because I am a consultant but because I can demonstrate the accuracy of my position, that contractors, agents, consultants, and people outside your company's employment often can be more effective because they have less to lose by being innovative, radical, direct, different, and bold.

apiece for the cleaned names and recovered $36,000 of its list rental cost of $160,000.

The Benefits of Predictive Dialing Systems

Every company is as unique as a thumbprint. But in one regard all companies are similar. They could be selling more product or selling it more profitably. I take quite seriously the notion that *selling* is one thing and *prospecting,* or finding noncustomers, is another thing. Many of us run companies or divisions whose salespersons know how to sell. That is, their close ratios (sales/prospects) are high. But many salespeople do not know how to prospect. They waste time at it but it is unfair to blame them. Most companies do not know how to find noncustomers inexpensively.

Thus, when a computer comes along that will tiptoe through a list of potential customers at speeds permitted by Intel's 486 chip-based personal computer system and find prospects for the telephone operators to qualify, then sell the names to the sales force at $10 per lead, a significant breakthrough has occurred in marketing.

The primary vendors of predictive dialing systems in the United States, along with other relevant information, are listed in Exhibit 2-1.

Affording a Predictive Dialing System

Recognizing that gratitude has a short shelf life, in the following sections of this chapter I will help you find the cash to pay for a predictive dialing system plus a ten-person telemarketing department to operate it. To generate the cash, we will hack away at the company's postage, fax, overnight courier, and E-mail costs. The key to achieving these savings is the word "ask." Providers will not reduce their charges unless you question the amounts. Providers of communications services have price structures ranging from high—for those customers who never question them—to low—for customers who ask for the best price, along with all the services that the communications company offers its largest customers.

Reducing Postage Costs

This section may seem like penny-ante stuff to you unless your company markets or locates customers via direct mail, a concept that

Exhibit 2-1. Vendors of predictive dialing systems.

Name	Code Number	Contact	Telephone Number
Digisoft Computers	Telescript	Peggy MacLean	212-289-0991
EXECUTONE Information Systems	———	Frank Rotatior	203-655-6500
Electronic Information Systems	———	Bob Schwartz	203-351-4800
InterVoice	RS#562	Director of Marketing	214-497-8862
Noble Systems	RS#576	James Noble, Sr.	404-851-1331
Ontario Systems	RS#580	Bill Young	317-284-7131
Results Telemarketing	RS#586	David Burton	800-284-5318
TeleDirect International	RS#591	Carol Smock	319-355-6440
TeleSystems Marketing	Spark	Barbara Magyar	703-385-1212

we explore in greater detail in Chapter 17. But the pennies, nickels, and dimes add up once you begin watching them. Here are some tips to save postage costs:

1. *Use an electronic scale* to avoid the need for adding extra postage "just to be safe."
2. *Use a postage meter*, rather than stamps, to limit your expense to the exact amount required.
3. *Use "Forwarding and Return Postage Guaranteed" and "Address Correction Required"* on all mail. This is a relatively inexpensive way to keep your mailing lists current.
4. *Use first-class presort when possible.* For those mailings that qualify, savings can be as much as 25%. More on presort later in this chapter.
5. *Use third-class bulk rates to save more than 60% for mailings of 200 pieces or more.* In addition, sorting by carrier routes eliminates three United States Postal Service handlings, allowing faster delivery. More on carrier route sorting later in this chapter.
6. *Include promotional pieces in your regular mailings of invoices and*

statements. Most letters mailed at the one-ounce rate weigh much less, so add a lightweight newsletter. More on this, also, in this chapter.

7. *Keep a variety of envelopes on hand, and always use the smallest possible size.* This lowers weight and avoids postage surcharges.

8. *Use registered mail only when insurance is necessary.* Certified mail is less expensive.

9. *For promotional mailings, use a first-class postcard, rather than a first-class letter.* A 4½″ × 6″ single-fold piece doubles your message area and can even accommodate a business reply card.

Profiting From Statement-Stuffer Programs

Think of your mailing envelope as a small but valuable piece of real estate within a shopping mall filled with marketers of products and services that complement yours and with customers and noncustomers who shop at your store and the others in this imaginary mall. *The envelope is a tollgate.* You are mailing something to a customer or to a noncustomer (prospects obtained from a list, rented or otherwise) although the probability that the recipient of your mailing piece will purchase the product or service that you are describing is quite slim, perhaps less than 5%.

You may not be stuffing as much as you can into the envelope at the lowest postage price the government will permit. You can test this yourself by walking into the mailroom with your mailing piece, an envelope, and several sheets of blank paper. Place your envelope and mailer on the postage scale. Let's say it registers 52 cents. Then add one sheet at a time until the postage meter goes up to the next price (74 cents). Pull the last sheet of blank paper off the scale. If the meter goes back to 52 cents with three sheets of blank white paper, then three is the number of additional mailing pieces that you can include in your envelope.

You can rent these three mailing pieces to three or more complementary companies that wish to reach your customers and noncustomers. This is gatekeeping—taking a cost center (the mailroom) and converting it to a profit center.

The Mechanics of Statement Stuffing

You actually have room for six or more marketing pieces on your three pieces of paper, thanks to two-sided printing. The object in operating the statement-stuffer tollgate is to pay for nothing and to collect the highest possible percent of the stuffees' (i.e., the cooperative manufacturers' or the service providers') sales dollars generated from your mailers. The typical stuffer commission is 30%.

It is imperative that the bounceback forms that appear on your stuffees' mailers be coded to indicate that your mailing list was used and that they be returned to a post office box that you control. If this is done, then you avoid both disputes and the need to audit the stuffees' books and records. Also, have your stuffees pay for the printing of their mailing pieces, and remind them to include a bounceback notice to your post office box and to code the bounceback. Select your stuffees on the basis of complementarity of their products or services with yours and on the affordability of their offering. Students of direct mail will tell you that products or services in the $60-to-$120 range produce the highest returns.

The most likely users of your mailing envelope are publishers of the industry's trade journals, seminar and trade show promoters, industry-related audio and video cassette publishers, providers of insurance to the industry, and other services such as employment agencies, long-distance telephone companies, and accounting firms. Producers of generic office equipment are eager to locate new and effective carrier pigeons to bring back purchase orders. Finally, producers of complementary products and services are good candidates for testing your mailing envelope and perhaps using it again in the future, depending on the payoff they obtain in the trial run.

Obviously, you could take the statement-stuffer idea to a higher level with something known as shared mail marketing. That topic is explored in Stage Three.

The Mathematics of Statement Stuffing

Here are some assumptions. Let's say you are going out with a 10,000-piece mailer to hospital and clinic administrators in North America to attempt to find prospects for your $2,500 software package and the computer system to run it on. You hope to generate 250 leads—a 2.5% response rate—and to close one-third of the leads with sales reps and a few salespersons in the field. The hoped-for revenues are 75 sales, or $187,500 in revenues, but you could live with $100,000.

Your mailing piece costs $10,000 to produce and print. The envelopes cost one penny apiece, or $100, and the postage costs 52 cents, or $5,200. Your total investment in this mailing piece is $15,300. The gross profit margin on your product is 65 percent. Your sales reps and salespersons receive a commission of 25 percent per sale.

Thus, on sales of five units, your cash flow statement on this one mailer is as follows:

Revenues	$100,000
Cost of goods sold	35,000
Gross profit	65,000
SG&A expenses:	
Commissions	− 25,000
Sales support, commissions	− 5,000
Mailing piece, postage	
(selling, general administrative)	− 15,300
Total SG&A expenses	45,300
Cash flow	$ 19,700

This gives you a 19.7% return on sales and a 40% return on investment. Not bad, but "not bad" is not why you are in business. You want to have some fun, put up some tollgates, and give your competition a run for its money. Therefore, you rent space in your mailing envelope to six complementary vendors. If each sells a $100 product, your piece of the pie (your envelope rental fee given a 30% commission) for three different response rates is shown in Exhibit 2-2.

For a 1% response rate, the statement-stuffer gatekeeping tactic generates $18,000, or slightly more than the SG&A costs of doing the mailer. If you do two 10,000-piece mailers a year and include six stuffee pieces that generate an average 1% response and an $18,000 commission, your total SG&A expenses increase from $15,300 to $21,600, since you do not have to redesign the mailing piece, and your commission income doubles to $36,000. At this point, your mailroom, assuming it has one full-time employee (whose salary is

Exhibit 2-2. Add-on revenues from renting your envelope to 6 stuffees.

Response Rates	1%	2%	3%
Units	100	200	300
Sales at $100	$10,000	$ 20,000	$ 30,000
× 6 vendors	60,000	120,000	180,000
× 30%	18,000	36,000	54,000

shared among three departments) at a cost for salary and benefits of $6,000 has become a profit center:

Revenues	$36,000
Less: Labor	6,000
SG&A expenses	21,600
Net cash flow	$ 8,400

By introducing the gatekeeper concept to your cost-eating mail room, you turn the costs of prospecting into a profit. We expand on this subject in Stage Three, but for now my task is to generate cash flow quickly and in a reliable and repeatable manner.

Utilizing Presorting Services

Should you become a heavy user of the U.S. Postal Service, you may want to familiarize yourself with presorting services. Major mailers, such as credit card companies and mail-order houses, sort their mail by zip code before taking it to the post office. The U.S. Postal Service offers them a 25% discount, or 4 cents off a 29-cent mailing. An independent government commission that reviews postal rates says that the presorting discount is a bargain. (Understandably, the American Postal Workers Union, a 350,000-member union, argues that its members could do the job just as well and would like to see 2.5 cents of the discount in their paychecks.)

But what about companies that generate 500 pieces of mail per day? If that is your situation, you can call on one of 250 privately owned presorters located throughout the country. Private presorters save you most of the four cents, which can add up to several thousand dollars per year, depending on volume.

Presorting by Carrier Route

If your company sends out thousands of third-class envelopes each month, or if it plans to, your postage costs are $167 per thousand pieces, or 16.7 cents per envelope. This assumes that you are presorting by zip code. You can lower the cost to $101 per thousand pieces, or 10.1 cents per envelope, a savings of 33%, if you sort the envelopes by carrier routes.

Regional post offices will provide you with the names of their carriers and the addresses they cover. Obtain census maps from the U.S. Commerce Department and enlarge them. Then hire high school students to sort the envelopes by carrier routes and have the students bundle the batches with rubber bands and write the name of the carrier on the top of each bundle. Then mail the bundles to the post offices.

Saving With Overnight Couriers

If your company is paying the highest rates for overnight delivery, then you are paying retail to support all the companies that have asked for wholesale prices. The retail rates for an overnight Federal Express, DHL, or Airborne Express letter is $14.00; for a one-pound package the rate is $20.25 to $25.00; and for a five-pound package, it is $31.25 to $34.00.

The overnight couriers that do not have the good fortune to count you among their customers would very much like to. No company ever has enough customers, including the overnight couriers. If you ask them for the discount that they give to IBM, AT&T, and Exxon, they will give it to you; if your volume is large enough, they may give you a free copier or another signing bonus. The discount is steep, approximately 40%:

Weight (lbs.)	Average Courier Wholesale Rate
Letter	$ 8.50
1	14.00
2	15.00
3	18.00
4	21.00
5	23.00
50	103.00

What does this mean in savings to your company? Let's say that your company ships 1,700 packages a year, or about six per day, and that the average weight is two pounds. If you are paying retail, your courier costs are about $39,100 per year. Once you change couriers and ask for the discount, your courier costs will drop 40% to $23,460, a savings of $15,640 per year.

If your volume of overnight packages is much smaller than that, you can still get the 40% discount by contacting an aggregator who collects many small-volume shippers and, with the power that large numbers brings, negotiates a steep discount for them. The best-known aggregator in the United States is UniShippers Association (telephone number 1-800-SHIPPERS).

Cutting Your Telephone Bills

There are several ways to reduce telephone costs. You can save by shopping for long-distance service and by purchasing your own equipment.

The Loneliness of the Long-Distance Phone Company

As you know, there are alternatives to AT&T as your company's primary long-distance carrier. The alternatives, as well as their fierce rival AT&T, fill the media with claims of lower cost, better clarity (or less noise), superior computer links, more fiber optic lines, and better conferencing. But these claims do not speak to the point. The point is price—which carrier offers the lowest rate per minute to use its telephone lines and equipment. Because price is an "in-your-face" way of marketing and not a palatable reason to switch for those customers who prefer to give the impression that quality of services is their prime motivator, the long-distance telephone carriers obfuscate the price issue with discounts, sign-up bonuses, affinity marketing schemes, gifts of office products, and frequent flyer points. In this environment, remember to ask for *all* of the benefits of switching and continue asking until you have been given as many as five "freebies."

The Advantages of Owning Your Telephone Equipment

If you replace rented telephone equipment with owned equipment, available at very low prices from telephone stores and electronics stores, you can achieve very significant savings. The cost saving features include least-cost routing, call accounting/cost accounting, and codes toll restriction, all of which are equipment-based features. Least-cost routing relies on a microchip embedded in the system that automatically selects the least costly carrier for a particular long-distance call. The call accounting/cost accounting feature automatically assigns the cost of a call to a specific client. Codes toll restriction automatically blocks certain telephones from calling certain area codes, preventing employees from making personal calls. According to telecommunications industry consultant Donn Thielman, president of Aztec Communications in Palm Desert, California, call accounting/cost accounting reduces monthly telephone bills by 30% and codes toll restriction slashes another 5%.

SCORECARD

We have piled up some serious cash in the communications area. Here is a summary:

• *Postage.* Let's assume that the $5 million (revenues) company spends $5,000 per month on postage and that the $20 million (revenues) company spends $20,000 per month on postage. With improved stuffing techniques and by paying more attention to using the full cost of the stamp, you achieve an out-of-pocket savings of 5%. Further, assume that, by using the monthly invoice as shelf space for your marketing piece, sales are increased 15% without adding overhead; the net cash flow on the sales increase is 20%. Thus, the scorecard for turning the mailroom into a partial tollgate is as follows:

	$5 million company	$20 million company
(a) Annual cash savings	$3,000	$12,000
(b) New sales (annualized)	9,000	36,000
(c) 20% of new sales	1,800	7,200
(d) Increased cash flow: (a) + (c)	$4,800	$19,200

• *Statement-stuffer programs.* The additional net cash flow that the two companies generate by renting space in their marketing mailers to six other vendors is estimated at $36,000 per mailout at a 2% response (in addition to the $19,200 net cash flow generated by sales of the company's products from its 100,000-piece mailer). For purposes of measuring the buildup in our pile of cash, let's assume that the smaller company mails to 400,000 addresses per annum at a 2% response rate and that the larger company mails to 1.6 million addresses. The net additional cash flow is as follows:

	$5 million company	$20 million company
Cash flow from own products/services—net	$ 78,800	$315,200
Cash flow from statement- stuffer program	144,000	576,000
Total cash flow	$222,800	$891,200

• Courier savings. It would be surprising to me if your company is paying list rate on its overnight courier service because the competition is quite heated and the delivery personnel are instructed to drop their prices as necessary. Therefore, in computing the scorecard, I will assume that you will pick up only $1.00 per overnight courier package by either asking for the reduction or through an affinity program. Accordingly, the net cash flow to the two sample companies is:

	$5 million company	$20 million company
Overnight packages/day	6	24
Overnight packages/year	15,000	60,000
Savings at $1.00/package	$15,000	$60,000

• *Telephone.* We will estimate the cash savings to be generated by asking the three major long-distance carriers to cut their rates, plus the cash savings to be derived by installing call accounting/cost accounting and codes toll restrictions at the low end of the reality spectrum—15% per annum. Assuming that the $5 million (revenues) company spends $3,000 per month in long-distance calls and the $20 million (revenues) spends four times that amount, or $12,000 per month, the scorecard flashes the following net cash savings:

	$5 million company	$20 million company
Cash savings per year	$5,400	$21,600

In summary, the communications areas within your company are rife with cash savings potential. Given the new features made possible by the microchip, the cash generating opportunities are positively riveting. With 30 to 60 days of intense focus on three areas—the mailroom, overnight courier service usage, and long-distance telephone service—we generated the following net new cash flow for our sample companies:

Box Score No. 2

Annual Net New Cash Flow

Area	$5 million company	$20 million company
Postage savings	$ 4,800	$ 19,200
Statement stuffer	222,800	891,200
Overnight couriers	15,000	60,000
Long distance telephone	5,400	21,600
Total	$248,000	$992,000

3

Slashing Health Care Insurance Costs

The health insurance costs borne by U.S. companies are staggering. As the Clinton Administration searches for solutions to these ever-rising costs, various medical industry groups are recommending voluntary price controls and other remedies. There are no easy answers. However, for companies that employ 25 to 250 people, some suggestions include spinning off various departments, converting some employees to independent contractors, and even instituting lay-offs. As these strategies downsize your total number of employees, some of the less expensive forms of health insurance become feasible. The two least expensive forms are (1) *self-insurance* with catastrophic-only coverage, and (2) *association-based group health insurance*. Not only is the latter inexpensive, its policyholders can earn a profit on it.

Health insurance is a personal matter. If each of us paid for insurance or for health care delivery if we chose not to buy insurance, then we would watch every penny very carefully, and the result would be falling rather than rising health care costs. But it is not our pocketbooks that foot the bill but our employers and our government, and like kids in a candy store we select the health plan that suits us best.

At my company, the plan that I selected for myself and the other employees and their families costs, on average, $196.50 per month per employee, and its features enable us to earn in cash about $356 per month per employee. We are not alone; hundreds of thousands of small businesses the size of mine are making money on their health care costs through association-based health insurance.

Entrepreneurs and Wellness

The actuarial tables on owners of small businesses and entrepreneurial companies suggest that they are the healthiest group of people in the country. "We don't get sick because we can't afford to be out," says Richards C. Thomas, founder and CEO of TEC Industries.

Entrepreneurship is business wellness. It is taking an idea and running with it. It is taking over a tired, overweight, bloated corporation and cutting the fat, trimming expenses, spinning off excess baggage, and running a lean, mean money machine. Entrepreneurship is wellness in action—problem solving, improving an outmoded practice, adding value, increasing employment, creating wealth. People who do this say they love the "chase." "I didn't leave the practice of dentistry and start a company to create wealth," says Dr. Barry M. Libin, founder of SYMAX Corporation, producer of a whitening toothpaste. "I did it for the chase."

Entrepreneurs and small-business owners are not the people you see jogging at 6:00 A.M. or during their lunch breaks. They are not doing the Stairmaster at the health spa or athletic club. Their wellness program is based on the chase.

But everyone cannot be an entrepreneur or a small-business owner, even though many corporate employees, managers, government workers, and attorneys will tell you that they would like to be. To emulate the entrepreneurs in body, if not in career choice, corporate employees invented the wellness revolution of the 1980s and joined spas in droves to exercise, jump, jog, get fit, and learn to eat right. The wellness revolution is personal entrepreneurship: taking over one's body, spinning off the fat, cutting out the carbos, getting to the muscle. The result is a healthier population of both corporate employees and entrepreneurs and small-business owners. Raiders, for the most part, are not into personal wellness because their focus is heavily geared to creating personal wealth, rather than objectivizing a social utility in their work.

Association-Based Group Health Insurance

Recognizing that owners of small businesses are the healthiest segment of the population, a handful of insurance industry entrepreneurs, each acting independently but making the discovery simultaneously about ten years ago, developed the concept of association-based group health insurance.

The association-based group health insurers, through large, captive sales forces, attempt to link large numbers of policyholders in an association. The health insurance purchasers are deemed a group by the state insurance commissioners and therefore pay lower rates than individual health insurance policy holders. The health insurance policy is fairly narrow in terms of coverage, has high deductibles, and is geared to paying catastrophic claims. The policy that covers my family and the other four employees in my firm pays for all hospitalization, including maternity, above a $2,500 deductible, plus dentistry from the first dollar. It does not pay for routine visits to the doctor. Nor does it pay for checkups and examinations. It is a lousy policy for people who are often sick, but like other small, entrepreneurial companies, we cannot afford to have an employee who misses work frequently.

Including myself, my company has five employees and 13 dependents. We pay $797.70 per month, or $9,572.40 per year, for health insurance. But we earn approximately $17,112 per year through the association.

The association is a classic gatekeeper. It collects $20 per policyholder per month out of the monthly insurance premium and uses the clout of its 65,000 members to negotiate significant discounts on travel, pharmaceuticals, eyeglasses, food, and other services. For example, let's say I fly to Boston from Albuquerque, rent an Alamo car, and stay two nights at the Omni Parker House Hotel. The association's discounts on these three travel services are:

Airline:	12%
Hotel:	50%
Car:	50%

If the airline ticket is $836.00, the hotel $370.00, and the car rental $188.00, my savings are shown in Exhibit 3-1.

Let's assume now that I, or someone in my firm, takes four trips per month that would cost approximately $1,324.00 at retail. The saving in travel costs per month then becomes $1,376.00. Add to this the discounts on food, pharmaceuticals, eyeglasses, legal services, and other items continually being added by the insurance company (an average of, let's say, $50.00 per month), and you can see that our health insurance policy pays us approximately $1,426.00 per month and costs us about $798.00 per month.

Thus, by being a small company with fairly healthy employees, we earn about $638.00 per month on our health insurance. These cash earnings can flow through to the employees or to the company's stockholders.

Exhibit 3-1. Travel discounts obtained through association-based health insurance.

	Price Full (Retail)	Discount	Price to the Insured
Airline	$ 836.00	12%	$100.32
Hotel	370.00	50%	185.00
Car Rental	118.00	50%	59.00
Total	$1,324.00		$344.32

Where Do You Sign Up?

Not every company may purchase association-based group health insurance. The policies are sold on an individual basis to companies of five or fewer employees. If you employ eight people, you cannot sign up all eight on the first pass. However, you can add employees later. Therefore, sign up five now, and "add" three later on. My company's policy, for example, permits us to add eight additional employees, until we reach a total of 13.

The names, addresses, and telephone number of the four leading association-based group health insurance companies in the country are as follows:

The Five Leading Association-Based Group Health Insurance Companies

National Health Insurance Co.
P. O. Box 619999
Grand Prairie, TX 75261-9999
1-800-237-1900

American Service Life Insurance Co.
200 Bailey
Fort Worth, TX 76107
1-800-366-5433

PFL Life Insurance Co.
4333 Edgewood Road, N.E.
Cedar Rapids, IA 52499
1-319-398-8511

Pioneer Life Insurance Co.
304 North Main
Rockford, IL 61101
1-815-987-5000

But everyone cannot qualify for association-based health insurance. What are the options for larger companies (besides splitting into dozens of five- to ten-person units)?

Managed Care

Managed care plans came on like gangbusters in the 1980s as an alternative to traditional indemnity plans. Health maintenance organizations (HMOs) and preferred provider organizations (PPOs) promised to reduce health care costs by encouraging the use of selected health care providers and discouraging unnecessary procedures.

Many companies went the managed care route and found that their *rate* of cost increases slowed, but not remarkably. A 1991 survey of 2,409 employees by the benefits consulting firm A. Foster Higgins & Co. found that the average cost of group health insurance per covered employee—including traditional medical plans, HMOs, dental plans, and prescription drug plans—was $3,605 in 1990, up from $2,748 in 1989 and more than double the 1985 average of $1,724 per employee.

The data do show, however, that, on average, HMOs are the lowest cost type of benefit plan. The nationwide per-employee cost for HMO coverage was $3,046, compared to $3,355 for PPO coverage and $3,573 for traditional indemnity plans. Still, the 1991 nationwide average per-employee rate for HMOs was 13.5% above the 1990 rate of $2,683. This does not speak well of the cost containment features of managed care plans.

The problem with managed care is that employees don't like it. According to the Higgins survey, 74% of the employees surveyed were offered managed care options, but only 45% of the employees chose to use them. The majority chose traditional indemnity coverage (55%). Of the remainder, 23% chose HMOs, and 17% selected PPOs. The failure of managed care as a cost-saving strategy is, in part, a result of the fact that employers offer it as an option and employees tend to reject it.

The primary negative brush with which all HMOs are painted is the inability of the patient to select the provider of his or her health care. Patients have to use the provider who has joined the HMO and agreed to the HMO's lower prices for health care. These providers are frequently unknown to the patients and are not the ones they would have selected if the choice had been up to them.

Another reason for HMOs' lack of popularity is that HMO

managements are clever marketers. They figure out what their potential clients spend on indemnity plans and put their prices 5 to 10% lower.

Your company's location also comes into play. Companies that have selected HMOs for their employees in the Pacific region paid on average $2,894 per employee in 1991; in New England, companies using HMOs paid an average $3,261. In Atlanta HMOs cost on average 4.8% less than indemnity plans, but in New York they cost 25% less.

In Atlanta, the PPO is the best buy. The PPO differs from the HMO in that the HMO acts like an insurance carrier while the PPO gathers large numbers of employees under its wing and then plays one insurer off against another until it negotiates the best rates. SouthCare Medical Alliance in Atlanta is one of the most successful PPOs in the country.

Lockheed-Georgia, a 20,000-employee subsidiary of the Lockheed Corporation, joined the SouthCare Medical Alliance PPO in 1988 and slashed its employee costs by $500,000, according to Donald Meader, coordinator of PPOs for Lockheed-Georgia. "We think that's only the beginning," Meader says. "We hope to do as well with dental, drugs, and therapy costs."

"The answer to delivering lower costs to employers via the PPO system," says Larry Madlem, who manages SouthCare, "is to deal with physicians as if they were travel agents and hospitals as if they were airlines. The smart physicians know they'll sell the most tickets if they deliver the lowest cost fares and offer prompt, efficient service. Once you have that understanding, the smart insurance companies—the ones without HMOs—will line up for your business."

Larry Madlem learned the employee health care business at John Deere, the Moline, Illinois, farm equipment manufacturer that dived headfirst into health care cost containment in 1971. Deere has its own insurance program and reinsurance company, and its health care costs per employee were $110 per month in 1988. When Madlem felt that he understood the health care financing problem and how he might provide an effective solution, he left Deere and formed SouthCare. In addition to Lockheed-Georgia, Madlem has signed dozens of corporations and institutions representing 150,000 insured employees from Atlantic Steel Corporation, the International Brotherhood of Electrical Workers, and the Glaziers Union.

For providers, SouthCare went after the lower-cost hospitals in Atlanta, primarily the not-for-profits, because they attract the lower-cost physicians. To qualify for membership in SouthCare, a provider must agree to bill at 15 to 20% less than the standard fee for a given procedure. An employee can go outside the SouthCare network to select his or her own physician, but SouthCare will pay only 80% of the fee.

Self-Insurance

Managed care was not the only technique pursued in the 1980s to reduce health care costs. Increasingly, companies trying to gain control of health care costs have opted to self-insure, while utilizing the same managed care techniques practiced by other companies. The Higgins survey found that 65% of the respondents to its 1991 survey self-insured; in 1986, fewer than half did.

In theory, self-insurance can reduce costs by eliminating the insurance company's profit margin. Many big employers believe they were effectively self-insuring even when they bought coverage because the claims and administrative costs of their benefits programs were built into the premiums they paid. And with hundreds of thousands of employees, big firms had a large enough risk pool to provide their own coverage.

In-House Medical Facilities

A few companies have taken self-sufficiency to an extreme by providing medical services for employees at in-house medical facilities. One such business, QuadGraphics, a Pewaukee, Wisconsin, printing company with a long history of self-sufficiency, recently built a clinic with a nine-physician staff that provides a full range of primary care services, including pediatric and OB/GYN care, as well as performing minor surgery; the clinic also features an on-site pharmacy and a full-service laboratory.

Gillette has provided an in-house medical facility for its Boston employees for more than 40 years and is considering expanding its role to serve employees' dependents, as well as employees. Goodyear now has four medical centers offering services to its employees. But, clearly, going into the health care business isn't an option for most companies.

In reality, self-insurance cuts costs only to the extent that the employer can administer a health benefits program less expensively than the insurer did—and only if it can negotiate at least as good a financial deal with medical providers. Obviously, small companies with few employees have much less negotiating clout with physicians, hospitals, and HMOs than do Fortune 500 companies.

Nevertheless, in recent years, many smaller companies have chosen to self-insure. The number of self-insured small businesses (employing 100 or fewer people) jumped to 22% in 1991, up from 8% in 1988.

One major attraction of self-insurance for smaller companies is that, to date, courts have held that self-insured companies are exempt from state insurance laws mandating the illnesses that insurers must cover. This exemption means that a self-insured employer can reduce or eliminate coverage that it would have to provide if it bought insurance from a third party.

A much publicized example is the case of Texas-based H&H Music. The company's insurance policy provided employees with up to $1 million of lifetime medical coverage. After one employee began filing claims for treatment for acquired immunodeficiency syndrome (AIDS), H&H Music changed to a self-insurance plan and imposed a $5,000 maximum lifetime limit for AIDS-related claims. The employee sued H&H Music for discrimination but lost the case when a federal appeals court ruled that the company was within its rights as a self-insured unit. If H&H Music had continued to buy insurance instead of self-insuring, the employee wouldn't have lost his coverage because Texas law forbids insurance companies to exclude coverage for AIDS.

SCORECARD

If your company employs 25 or fewer people, you may be able to cut your work force to fewer than a dozen employees and qualify for association-based group health insurance rates. You can also advise all 25 employees that you are cancelling the company's health insurance and that they are each free to buy an association-based (or some other) policy on their own. You can give them raises equal to the amount of their insurance payment.

If you are able to spin off the sales department of your company into an independent contracting firm of five or fewer people and have them self-insure with an association-based group health insurance company, everyone will come out a winner. (I propose that you do some things like that in Stage Two.) But, for now, let's assume that by shopping for a PPO or by otherwise merging your personnel with a large association that negotiates savings in health insurance costs, a 10% annual savings is achieved.

Box Score No. 3

Health Insurance

	$5 million company	*$20 million company*
Number of employees (at $110,000 in sales per employee)	45	180
Annual health insurance cost @ $250/ month	$135,000	$540,000
Savings at 10%	$ 13,500	$ 54,000

4

Rolling Back Legal Expenses

Question: What do you call 500 lawyers at the bottom of the ocean?

Answer: A beginning.

Company owners habitually call their lawyers to handle routine problems that fly about like dust in the air—bad debts, leases, disputes, loan agreements. Many company owners retain law firms on an ongoing basis whether they need legal assistance or not. And many children take their security blankets to college with them. One does about as much good as the other.

The principal reason that we use lawyers is that governments are run by lawyers and they have elected not to print and publish the rules and regulations for representing oneself in the courts. By keeping the laws and the rules for using the laws hidden, the government's lawyers make sure that the average citizen feels that he or she must hire a lawyer as a seeing eye dog. The problem with this is that lawyers live and breed their young in Disputesville and Troubletown, and they perpetuate conflict, rather than resolution.

All lawyers are not *cathartidae*, and not all business owners are naive about lawyers. But enough are to have driven legal expenses for most companies to the moon.

My sangfroid about being sued and suing is the result of 20 years of putting together venture capital for entrepreneurs, acquisition capital for leveraged buyouts, and rescue capital for workouts and turnarounds. There is always a lawyer somewhere who can be hired to sue someone by a person who either has been made angry or who sees an opportunity to extort money from a plausibly innocent defendant by giving him motion sickness, deposition disease, and/or suing him with a host of embarrassing charges and then publishing the lawsuit in the defendant's local newspapers and trade journals.

In the venture capital and investment banking business, where not every deal pays back its investors, you can pretty much count on being sued with some frequency. This does not mean that the risk capital industry is populated with dishonest people. Rather, the water in the pond in which we investment bankers play is stocked with sharks.

Let me tell you a story. An entrepreneur, an accountant, and a lawyer once sailed out of Miami into the Caribbean, when their sail was torn off by high winds and their engine stopped cold. When their food ran out two days later, the three men discussed how they would try to save themselves. They were only a mile or so from a populated island, but the water was infested with sharks whose dorsal fins could be seen circling the troubled boat.

The entrepreneur spoke first.

"I will use my enormous powers of persuasion to persuade the wind to blow us in."

He tried, but failed. The accountant spoke next.

"I will precisely measure our distance from shore and the time I think it will take for someone to find us."

Nothing happened. So the lawyer spoke.

"I will dive into the water and swim to the island and bring back help."

The entrepreneur and the accountant asked him, almost in unison, "But what about the sharks?"

Before he could answer them, the lawyer dived into the sea. The sharks lined up on either side of him and circled him but they did not bother him. Within a few hours the lawyer returned on a rescue boat with help.

"Why did the sharks not bother you?" the accountant asked when he and the entrepreneur were finally safe.

"Professional courtesy," answered the lawyer.

Flat-Fee Billing

According to a study by Robert Litan of the Brookings Institution and Steven Salop of Georgetown University, the revenues of the legal profession have grown from 1966 to the present at a rate of 12% per annum, or faster even than health care insurance costs.

Moreover, in a study published in the *Rutgers Law Review* in 1991, William Ross, a professor of the Cumberland School of Law, wrote that, of 272 attorneys he surveyed, 60% admitted that they were aware of bill padding in their offices.

Bickel & Brewer, a 43-attorney law firm based in Dallas that specializes in complex corporate litigation, has changed its billing practice to primarily individually negotiated flat-fee work. If the firm achieves a better result for its client than had been originally expected, it receives a performance bonus, also negotiated in advance. Ross, in his *Rutgers Law Review* article, reports that hourly billing not only leads to bill padding and unnecessary and duplicative work— Ross reports that one in five of the lawyers he surveyed believes that it is ethical to bill a client for research or other work originally done for another client and recycled—but discourages the use by lawyers of productivity-improving technology.[1]

Legal excesses have brought into being the legal bill checker industry. In 1988 John Marquess founded Legalgard, which scrutinizes legal bills for clients such as Liberty Mutual Insurance, Mattel, and the state of New Jersey. Marquess's business is booming. Revenues tripled each year from 1987 to 1992, reaching $3.6 million in 1992.

Marquess does not believe that flat-fee billing is the solution. "Any flat fee must allow for a giant margin," he argues.[2] However, flat-fee billing does eliminate the problem inherent in hourly billing— the tendency to stretch out the job.

When You Are Sued

To protect your company from the ravages of a contingency-fee lawyer who sues your senior management and board of directors on behalf of an employee for wrongful failure to promote, for departure from policies spelled out in company employment booklets, or for giving a bad reference for a terminated employee, I recommend that you explore the purchase of directors and officers errors and omission liability insurance, known as D&O insurance. It may cost your company $5,000 to $6,000 per year, but it prevents your having to write a six-figure check to settle a nuisance lawsuit. In addition, you may not be able to attract a first-class board of directors without D&O insurance.

Do not treat this subject blithely, particularly if your company is located in California. A recent survey found that California employer defendants lose 78% of all lawsuits against corporations that go before juries, at an average verdict of $424,527. A worker fired for refusing a drug test, for example, was awarded $480,000. A survey by Rand Corporation researchers found that wrongful-dismissal cases brought an average of $646,000 at trial. A national survey by the Bureau of

National Affairs found the average age-discrimination verdict to be
$722,000.[3]

Some of the principal carriers of D&O insurance are listed in
Exhibit 4-1.

The Damage Trail

Immediately upon being sued, assign a loyal, meticulous employee—
let's call her the Lion—to maintain a damage trail: a chronological
listing of the damaging events that result from aggressive litigation.
Lawsuits are filed with public courts, and anyone, including reporters, has access to them. In fact, many newspapers station people full-
time in the courts to collect stories of disputes and disagreements
that become news a day or two later. Other self-appointed watchdogs
then photostat the stories and send them to the defendant's customers or vendors in other cities and to national publications. Before the
debtor company knows it, the inability to pay a vendor or a lender
becomes a lawsuit filed under antiracketeering laws and described in
minute detail in trade journals and national newspapers.

National and trade publications usually investigate the local
dispute more thoroughly and will telephone a spokesperson for your
company as well as for the plaintiff before printing an article. The
Lion should be the person who fields those telephone calls, and she
should be trained in the appropriate response. Many libel lawyers
advise you not to contribute to the article; statements only make it

Exhibit 4-1. Principal underwriters of D&O Insurance.

Aetna Life & Casualty
American International Group
Aon
British-American Insurance Group
Casualty Underwriters
Dearborn Insurance Co.
Great American Insurance Co.
Insurance Innovators Group
Interstate Insurance Management
Lexington Insurance Co.
National Union Fire Insurance Co.
Phoenix Excess & Surplus Lines
Seabord Underwriters
Tudor Insurance Co.

worse, they say. The plaintiff or its counsel is likely to make a statement to the trade journal or national publication, for it would be hard pressed not to answer the question, "What is the substance to your claim of racketeering?" The response might be something like, "We found several instances of misappropriation of money and accounting irregularities."

That is a damaging statement, and the Lion should enter it in the damage trail notebook. A large customer may read the article and tell the debtor company that it cannot do business with it any further until the charges made by the plaintiff are cleared up. The Lion should ask the customer for a letter to that effect to prove a direct causal relationship between the plaintiff's statement and the loss of business. The customer's letter then is filed in the damage trail notebook.

Other companies may refuse to service the defending company after reading the article. Credit card companies may send cancellation notices for their cards; banks may shut down the company's accounts; other vendors may stop shipping except on a COD basis. The Lion should dutifully record all of these events in the damage trail notebook. They will form the basis of counterclaims for damages arising from the plaintiff's statements to the press. These counterclaims may take the form of libel, tortious interference, business interference, and more. Pursuing the counterclaim will require expensive, experienced litigation lawyers and months of work compiling depositions and documents, but it puts litigants on notice that their cannons did not knock out yours.

Whether you pursue your causes of action to trial depends on the merits of your case, the predilections of the judge, and the amount of cash you can raise to stay the battle. In many instances, if the defendant company can build a hefty litigation war chest, it can negotiate a settlement and withdrawal of the damaging litigation with a powerful counterclaim. If the company doesn't have the cash both to pursue litigation and to sustain business operations, its enemies may prevail. In the litigation battlefield, soldiers march on cash.

Restraining Overzealous Creditor Lawyers

There were approximately 750,000 attorneys in the United States in 1991, and the nation's law schools are graduating 35,000 new ones a year. With so many lawyers needing to justify their existence and to feed their families, the frequency of litigation is skyrocketing. That's the bad news. The good news is that there are ways to bring overreaching lawyers to their knees.

The Federal Rules of Civil Procedure is pretty much the bible for how a lawsuit must be conducted in the federal courts (each state has its own version of Fed. R. Civ. P., as the lawyers refer to it). Any lawyer who violates these rules without justification may be sanctioned by the presiding judge.

Remember that if you overreach and misstate facts in seeking sanctions against an opposing attorney, you may be subject to the same penalties for which you are seeking redress. Furthermore, your attorney may not wish to file a motion for sanctions against another attorney, for they belong to a professional fraternity and tend to respect one another, despite aggressive behavior that is tantamont to lying. Thus, if you feel strongly that a creditor's attorney has caused you economic injury, you may have to file the motion for sanctions in your own name, or pro se.

The federal rules against which you must measure the violations to see if they are sanctionable are as follows:

> *Rule 11:* Any attorney or other person admitted to conduct cases in any court of the United States or any Territory thereof who so multiplies the proceedings in any case unreasonably and vexatiously may be required by the court to satisfy personally the excess costs, expenses, and attorneys' fees reasonably incurred because of such conduct.

Rule 11 is used primarily when opposing counsel causes you to spend time and money needlessly by requesting multiple documents and multiple depositions or by making false statements that you must take time and spend money to correct.

> *Rule 37:* This provision places the burden on the disobedient party to avoid expenses by showing that his failure was justified.

Rule 37 may be invoked if the court issues an order that the opposing counsel disobeys. Penalties are stiffer under Rule 37 than under Rule 11 because a court order has been violated. The rule may apply if a creditor sues your company for nonpayment of a debt, and you seek through the court to determine if the amount shown as owed on the creditor's accounts receivable ledger is actually the true amount. Differences can arise if there is a service contract is involved or if goods or parts were shipped back because of defects. If the creditor refuses to allow access to its records, you can request the records in a deposition. If the creditor blocks the deposition or gives insufficient information at the deposition, you can then seek an order to have the information provided to you forthwith.

> *Rule 26(g):* Provides for sanctions against an attorney if he seeks to increase your costs of litigation "for any improper purpose, such as to harass or to cause unnecessary delay or needless increase in the cost of litigation." False statements, improper motions filed against you for harassment purposes, and other actions by opposing counsel that increase expenses needlessly are plausibly actionable under Rule 26(g).

The Benefits of Pro Se

Because your counsel is unlikely to throw bricks at a colleague, perhaps you should think about representing yourself. By acting pro se, you will save thousands of dollars and probably do as well as if you hired counsel. (This is not true in bankruptcy. A debtor *must* be represented by counsel in Chapter 11 proceedings.)

A good reason for representing yourself in the litigation aspects of a collection dispute is that it renders creditors' counsel somewhat helpless, or at least uncertain as to how you are likely to respond in certain circumstances. Lawyers know how lawyers relate to one another, but they do not know how a businessperson will respond in every circumstance. Acting pro se is a Sun Tzu-derivative strategy: You get inside the opponent's head and upset the form and rhythm that the opponent typically follows to collect a debt.

A third reason for a pro se defense is that any lawyer you are likely to hire will think within the constructs of his or her legal training but probably not strategically. Assume, for example, that a creditor hires the law firm of Jones, Smith & Doe to represent it in collecting a $1 million debt that your company legitimately owes but cannot pay without a standstill agreement of 90 to 120 days followed by a four-year stretchout. The creditor wants its money now, and Jones, Smith & Doe comes at the company with all guns firing at once. They are sure to gain the upper hand because they have more money with which to fight a sustained battle.

In the course of your company's many years in business, however, you have used Jones, Smith & Doe to represent your company in another matter. To interrupt the $1 million collection process, you raise the firm's alleged conflict of interest with the disciplinary commission of the state bar association (in some instances, the State

Supreme Court) in the state in which your company has been sued, asking that the disciplinary commission remove the Jones firm because it has represented you in the past. You may win the argument; in any event, the creditor is forced to back off until the matter is resolved. The disciplinary commissions of the various states are empowered to resolve disputes between clients and the law firms that pay the disciplinary commissioners' salaries, which tells you right up front that your company is unlikely to obtain a balanced ruling. But I have found that the disciplinary commissions try to be fair as long as the alleged infraction that you bring to their attention is legitimate.

Some lawyers occasionally cross the line between bold advocacy and breaches of ethics. Some overprescribe, misdiagnose, or underperform. When this happens, ask your state's bar association or disciplinary commission to intervene. Neither agency can grant monetary relief, but they do have considerable power. The degree to which they can punish offending law firms is shown in Exhibit 4-2.

A word of warning, however: The law firms in each state pay fees to these two state referees, fees that provide them with the wherewithal to hire staff and serve the public. Like most regulatory agencies, the referees of legal disputes follow the economist Milton Friedman's law, which states that regulatory agencies, to justify their existence, support the industry they are empowered to regulate. Just remember—the layperson is *not* the client of the bar associations and disciplinary commissions.

Achieving Additional Reductions in Legal Costs

You have many options to consider as you seek to cut your legal bills. Here are a few of them.

• *Use your lawyers efficiently.* Most companies use their lawyers inefficiently. For example, when a firm sends a team of lawyers to explain a legal problem, the company's employees fail to ask two of them to leave the room. The scope of the legal services required can usually be determined by one lawyer in less than 30 minutes of billable time. In addition, most companies do not put their legal requirements out for bid and then interview many lawyers at different firms. Nor, when someone refers a lawyer to the company, do they ask why this lawyer, in particular, is the best choice. For all they know, the person making the referral may be earning psychological or social points but may not be putting the company into the best

Exhibit 4-2. Powers of bar association disciplinary bodies.

Disbarment: The lawyer may be disbarred and prohibited from practicing law in the state. Disbarment usually is imposed for criminal actions or gross misconduct bordering on crime.

Suspension: The lawyer may be suspended from practicing law for a period ranging from one day to several years, depending on the nature of the improper conduct.

Public Reprimand: The lawyer may be sanctioned by the highest court in the state, and the sanction may be cited in the newspaper.

Private Reprimand: This is the lightest of wrist slaps, intended only to establish a record for reference in the event of further misbehavior.

Source: American Bar Association

legal hands. It's always wise to probe for the reasons behind the referral.

• *Control the billing.* Discuss billing rates before engaging a lawyer or a firm. Discuss the way in which you wish to be billed—on a contingency basis, at an hourly rate with payments due each month, or per event. Many lawyers prefer that you pay a retainer up front—bankruptcy lawyers quite properly want 90% of their expected fee in advance—and then work the retainer off in hours. This is an appropriate arrangement for a complicated lawsuit or for a matter that has an uncertain ending, such as an acquisition or a public offering. It is inappropriate for the drafting of a contract. Prepare a budget with your lawyer before the task begins, and monitor the budget.

Be sure to specify that you want fully itemized bills that break down each hour or fraction thereof and that describe how the time was spent. Question billed items that you don't understand or accept. For example, your lawyer does not have to travel first-class. If he or she does not work for you while traveling, he or she should not bill you for travel time.

Roy H. Park, the innovator of Duncan Hines days and now the owner of broadcast properties and newspapers, recommends telephone calls rather than visits to lawyers. He keeps a "talk sheet" by the telephone, invites members of management into the room, and puts the lawyer on the speaker phone. When the conversation is over, the time is noted and the talk sheet is typed and filed in the legal costs folder, where it can be compared with the lawyer's monthly bill when it arrives.

• *Consider using in-house legal talent.* If your company consistently spends more than $75,000 a year on legal fees, it is time to consider hiring in-house counsel. However, most in-house lawyers can't handle the "big case," specialized issues—environmental, tax, securities, antitrust—or litigation away from home.

If in-house counsel can contribute to other functional areas, such as corporate finance or fundraising, you may get two tasks filled by the same person. Legal training is intensely analytical, and many lawyers are excellent acquisition analysts and financial planners.

• *Consider shifting to small, low-overhead firms.* General Motors recently reviewed the results obtained by its law firms and found "some less than stellar results," according to Harry J. Pearce, vice president and general counsel.[4] As a result, GM shifted a lot of its legal work to smaller firms with lower overheads.

One small but telling example involves an arrangement between General Motors and Chukwuemeka N. Chionuma, a Kansas City, Missouri, lawyer. The deal calls for GM to funnel all breach-of-warranty cases filed by dissatisfied car buyers to Mr. Chionuma's nine-lawyer firm. In return, the firm, North & Chionuma, charges the company a predetermined flat fee, rather than a traditional hourly rate. The cost to GM on each case is the same whether the case takes a month or a year to settle or to try.

The law firm generally handles about eight to ten breach-of-warranty cases for GM at any given time. "With the volume of work that was assigned to us, we were able to propose and maintain a flat rate that is substantially below what our hourly bill would have been," says Mr. Chionuma. GM has worked out similar arrangements with other legal vendors, including firms in Minneapolis and New York, for product-liability cases and for other litigation.

• *Negotiate alternatives to traditional hourly billing. There are several popular alternatives to traditional law firm billing practices. They include:*

• *Volume discounts.* The company agrees to refer all of a specific kind of work to a law firm in exchange for discounted fees.

• *Blended rates.* Clients pay a single hourly rate for the work of senior and junior lawyers alike, thereby encouraging law firms to staff cases efficiently.

• *Flat fees.* The law firm handles matters for a preestablished price, no matter how many hours are required to complete the project.

• *Hourly rate discounts.* Regular billing rates are cut for the client.

• *Bidding*. A client invites several law firms to bid on a piece of work, detailing strategy, staffing plans, and fees.

• *Modified contingency fees*. A portion of the law firm's fee is pegged to its success in the case.

• Try cooperation as a strategy. Another method for mitigating the cost of litigation is to band together with companies in your region of the country and jointly refuse to hire any law firm that has a department that sues companies for product liability or racketeering, two of the most punitive forms of civil litigation and the kind that frequently leads to huge jury awards.

You can also cooperate with your competitors to keep disputes out of the courtroom and move them into the conference room. Competitors including General Mills, Kellogg, and Ralston Purina have signed a pact promising to mediate trademark, packaging, and marketing disputes that arise among them. Cliff L. Whitehill, general counsel of General Mills, says the group hopes that an additional 50 food companies will eventually sign the pledge. Similarly, a group of franchisers has signed a pledge promising to mediate disputes with its franchisees. Participants in this agreement include PepsiCo's Pizza Hut, McDonald's and Burger King, a unit of Grand Metropolitan PLC.

The food industry pledge calls for companies to try to mediate problems that can't be solved in 30 days without a neutral go-between. If the dispute is not settled after a mediator has been involved for at least 60 days, the parties can resort to the usual courtroom melees. Mr. Whitehill says that high litigation costs are not the primary motivation for the move toward mediation. The food companies are more worried that they will lose consumer goodwill if product packaging and marketing strategies must be altered after lengthy court battles. Fast resolutions are key, he says, because "business moves faster than the courts do."[5]

SCORECARD

Let's assume that your company's cost of legal services is quite small and that you have no material litigation to speak of. But you may in the future, and that is why you need to be alert should some lawyer start to shoot your lights out. Don't let him do it. Reverse the leverage on him. Tollgate him. Haul his pin-striped carcass in front of the state disciplinary commission from the outset of the litigation, and keep it there until he begins to act responsibly.

The Legal Fees Scorecard

Legal fees vary from year to year, depending on the kind and amount of trauma and upset a company goes through. A heavy legal expense year might be one that involves signing a loan or a purchase agreement, suing a customer for nonpayment of an invoice, being sued by a former employee, signing a lease, joint-venturing with a foreign supplier, and creating an employee profit-sharing plan. These legal "moments" can cost between $10,000 and $20,000 apiece, or $60,000 to $120,000 per year.

On the other hand, a light legal expense year might cost one-fifth of that amount, or $12,000 to $24,000 per year. It is difficult to predict when and how many disputes will need resolution, barricades will need hoisting, or contracts will need signing in the course of a year. However, for many of these matters, the company does not need a lawyer. Here is my idea of the scorecard.

Box Score No. 4

Legal Fees

	$5 million sales company	$20 million sales company
Leases	$ 5,000	$10,000
Notes	5,000	10,000
Collectors	10,000	20,000
Suits	—	10,000
Total legal expenses	20,000	50,000
Savings	$10,000	$25,000

Notes

1. David From, "Piecework," *Forbes* (February 15, 1993), p. 132.
2. Ibid.
3. Ellen Jane Pollock, "In a Bid to Trim Costs, Many Companies Are Forcing Law Firms to Reduce Fees," *The Wall Street Journal* (December 4, 1991), p. B-1.
4. Ibid.
5. Ellen Joan Pollock, "Food Concerns Opt to Meditate, Not Litigate," *The Wall Street Journal* (February 11, 1992), p. B-1.

5

Are Your Advertising Costs Out of Line?

Your company does not have to advertise at its current level. I am going to try to persuade you that sales leads can be generated less expensively, that customer response can be measured and weighed using the customer's money, and that sales can be achieved through word-of-mouth or testimonial selling. One must always bear in mind the distinction between finding potential customers (lead generation) and selling the prospects (marketing). The primary function of advertising is to generate leads. It is when a product's utility cannot easily be distinguished from the utility of its competitors that advertising plays a marketing role.

Why does your company advertise its products or services? Is it to generate leads (or, as some people say, "to achieve product identity") or is it to generate sales? The philosopher John Dewey said that the most important statement a person can make is to point a finger. Even without voices and most other common forms of communication, one can often communicate or answer a query by pointing.[1] Dewey states that advertising is our society's pointing finger.

Confusion reigns when many fingers point even though consumers have not been asked any questions. Buy this, try that, taste this, eat that, drink this, drive that, and so on—to toss your advertisements into this cacophonous din is to waste a fortune. For several years Federal Express wasted millions of dollars of investors' capital on advertisements that did not answer consumer concerns. First it hired Opinion Research Corporation, a national market research firm in Princeton, New Jersey, to evaluate the relative performance of five air freight services between twenty-four pairs of cities for two weeks in 1975. The study showed that Federal Express was faster and 40% less expensive and had a superior package-tracking capability.

How did Federal Express convert these data into a message for the marketplace? One of its ads read, "If you're using Emery, don't let your boss see these figures," with a display of the test results in the text. This message was ineffective and wasteful.

Federal Express next stressed that it was so efficient because it used its own planes, whereas Emery, Airborne, Purolator Courier, and others used commercial airlines. Its ad campaign read, "Take away our planes and we'd be just like everybody else." That was also a yawn. The marketplace didn't care how packages were shipped; it cared about when they were received.

Finally, in the late 1970s, the Federal Express marketing department realized that dependability was the key point. It developed the slogan "Absolutely, positively overnight" and put it across with humorous ads that relieved the anxiety of middle managers and shipping clerks whose jobs were on the line if a certain package did not get to Peoria the next day.

The Federal Express advertising failure derived from its mistaken belief that the customer was as proud of Federal's competitive advantages and company-owned airplanes as it was. This is called *centripetal thinking*. Being proud of one's product or service and its competitive advantages has its place. But it doesn't belong in advertising. The potential consumers of your product or service want to know *how* it solves their need. It's the John Dewey finger point: the universal response to a critical question in a world without voices or language. The key to effective advertising is to perceive the unvoiced question and deliver the correct finger point. There is an inexpensive way to find the need.

But We Cannot Slash Advertising

Yes you can. Let's assume that one of the places you advertise is in magazines and that you buy 50 magazine pages per year straight off the rate card at $30,000 per page. Further, assume that your company sells a service such as insurance, financial planning, or computer-based services to self-employed individuals or owners of small businesses or managers of medium-size and large corporations—a universe of about 35 million potential buyers. Moreover, assume that a 2% response rate to your magazine advertisements, which are coded by magazine, have typically produced 800,000 bounceback cards from prospects; that these cards are sorted and sent out to your agents or sales reps, who typically convert 5% of the prospects to sales; and that each sale brings in $500 to the company, for a total of $20 million per annum. Your company develops leads through other channels as well, but the 50 ads—an investment of $1 million per year—have produced, at least in the advertising manager's mind, 13.5 times the investment and therefore should not be tampered with.

You protest. The agent or sales rep receives a 50% commission, the costs of delivering the service (if it is insurance, the statutory reserve) is 35%, the general and administrative costs—handling, sorting, and mailing the leads and putting new account information into the computer—are $2 million per annum, and the advertising costs are $1.5 million. So just how profitable is this lead-generating and marketing channel?

Revenues	$20,000,000
Cost of sales or reserve	7,000,000
Sales commissions	10,000,000
General & administrative expenses	2,000,000
Advertising	1,500,000
Total expenses	20,500,000
Net profit or (loss)	$ (500,000)

What should you do? You can demand a 33% reduction in price per page from the magazine and get it by paying for the full 12 monthly issues up front. Even better, you can demand a 50% reduction in price per page if you buy two pages in each of the 12 monthly issues and pay for all 24 pages up front. Why would you do that? To barter or sell the 12 pages tht you don't need for 25% off the rate card, thus saving $7,500 for each page you barter or sell times 12 (the number of issues), or $90,000 per year. And, if you do the same thing—buy twice the pages you need for $15,000 and sell half of them for $22,500—in all four magazines that you regularly advertise in, you will earn $360,000 in additional cash flow. That, plus your savings in advertising, puts your advertising program comfortably in the black.

Revenues	$20,000,000
Barter income	1,080,000
Total revenues	$21,080,000
Cost of sales or reserve	7,000,000
Sales commissions	10,000,000
General & administrative expenses	2,000,000

Advertising	<u>1,500,000</u>
Total expenses	<u>20,500,000</u>
Net profit	$ <u>580,000</u>

By thinking like a gatekeeper and controlling 24 pages of advertising in four magazines, you have flipped a $500,000 loss into a $580,000 gain. If you cannot find advertisers for the 48 pages that you own, you have four choices:

1. Hire an advertising broker to find advertisers and pay him or her a 10% commission.
2. Put another version of your ad in the space, or experiment with a two-page spread.
3. Barter the pages to other companies that can provide you with important and expensive services.
4. Barter some of the pages, and resell the others.

Let's look at the fourth option in detail. Your company uses lawyers, accountants, airline tickets, hotel beds, telephone lines, and other services, for which it pays hard dollars. Probably most, if not all, of these service providers advertise, and some of them buy magazine pages because magazines are read by multiple readers, sit around in waiting rooms, and have been proved to be effective media.

You are sitting with 48 magazine pages for which you paid $15,000 apiece, or $720,000. Let's say you sell 24 of the pages for $22,500 each, or $540,000, and barter the remaining 24 pages for services. After all, you have a profit in your *core* advertising program, and your exposure has been reduced to $360,000 of pages worth $720,000 at their published rates. Here is what you bargain for:

- $144,000 of airline tickets without restrictions on one of the major carriers to be used by any of your company's employees at any time.
- $144,000 of accounting services and tax planning assistance from your accounting firm, to be used within two years.
- $144,000 of paper supplies in the stock and quality you choose.
- $144,000 of printing services.
- $72,000 of hotel beds to be used at any time without restriction by corporate employees.
- $36,000 of car rentals to be used at any time by corporate employees.

- $36,000 of overnight courier credits to be used to ship enve-
  lopes and freight anywhere at the full discounted rate you have
  been receiving.

Total barter value: $720,000

Now look at the *cash flow* of the advertising program:

Revenues	$20,000,000
Barter income	540,000
Savings in services	720,000
Total revenues	$21,260,000
Cost of sales or reserve	7,000,000
Sales commissions	10,000,000
General & administrative expenses	2,000,000
Advertising	1,500,000
Total expenses	20,500,000
Net profit	$ 760,000

With shrewd bargaining and clever bartering, you have turned
an operation with a $500,000 loss into one with a $760,000 profit—a
swing of $1,260,000—without tampering with the company's golden
hen—its advertising program.

Public Relations

An alternative to advertising is public relations, which involves generating interesting articles about your product or service in local and
national media. Magazine and newspaper articles sit around awhile,
are passed around, and are read by many people, and the information in them is retained to a far greater degree than is common for
the information in an advertisement.

Testing the publicity ability or "newsworthiness" of your new
product or service in advance with journalists can be a riveting
experience. Some of the journalists you meet—and a competent
public relations agent can arrange several such meetings—may tell
you that the product or service is not of interest and that nobody will
want to read about it.

That's when you *ask*. Probe to find out how to make it into a story. The journalists will respond from the consumer's viewpoint. Consumers want to save money. They want to relieve anxiety. They want to feel wealthier.

I urge you to take copious notes, because what you hear will help you write copy for your product and service. It is important that you attempt to write your own copy, mixing the significant points with the fluff so that the article gives the appearance of balanced reporting. By doing the writing yourself, you can determine the degree of difficulty in projecting the most desirable image of your product or service. Buy a handful of lively magazines and newspapers, such as *People*, *The National Enquirer*, and *Spy*, and study their upbeat writing styles and mainstream sentence configuration.

Publicity

When you're preparing your news release, have some consideration for the newspapers to which you send your press releases. They are more likely to run your articles if it does not cost them very much to edit or rewrite them and to adjust the accompanying photographs.

With the quality of desktop publishing and the multiple fonts available, you can write the article, squeeze it to a column width, create your own headline, insert a column-width glossy photograph, and send it on its way. The newspaper can then proofread, insert, and run it with minimal editorial cost.

What will this kind of consumer research cost you? Perhaps a fee of $500 per national media article published, payable to the public relations agent, and a few meals with journalists. What will it gain you? When you rewrite the press release, probably three to five articles.

When your salespeople go on the road to call on customer prospects they always have some dead time. For instance, if the first sales call is at 10:00 A.M., the hour between 9:00 and 10:00 A.M. can be used in a remarkably productive way.

The salesperson can call on the business reporter for the local newspaper and provide her with a story about your company, the problems that its products solve, and the uniqueness of its solutions. Perhaps there is a local tie-in; minimally, the salesperson can say, "I have been calling on potential customers in the area." The salesperson can leave a PR kit, some glossy photographs, and a silver dollar or other premium to remind the reporter of the company.

Then, in a couple of days, when the customer on whom the salesperson called needs outside validation of the product, she will see a positive story in the local newpaper. If that person's boss asks if she saw the article on that new machine in the local paper, she can say, "Yes, and I met with the company as well. Would you like to go over their proposal with me?"

Local PR is a strong endorsement, but to get it requires planning. Your marketing support staff must locate the name of the local newspapers (there are directories of these) and the name of the business or relevant reporter, and the visit must be scheduled. Newspaper offices are frequently located downtown, whereas salespeople are not. Thus, as a timesaver, the reporter should be invited for breakfast at the salesperson's hotel.

The impact made by dozens of articles in dozens of local newspapers just as your sales staff fans out across the country can be significant. The articles can generate orders; moreover, journalists' questions can help the marketing department position the product. If the salespersons are instructed to take notes on journalists' questions, the marketing department will have some interesting market research to sort through.

Remind the salespeople to send thank-you notes to the reporters. The sales force may visit those towns again someday.

Catalog Testing

You can do some very interesting market research for consumer products by placing your product in several direct mail catalogs. The product's photograph and descriptive information will appear on a third to a half of a page, which will be seen by millions of people. Some of them will order the product.

You want as much information about these purchasers and their reactions to your product as you can obtain. The catalog company will provide you with their names and addresses. You can then telephone them and interview them about the product. You'll learn more than you ever imagined about uses, needs, and problems associated with the product.

CEO Testing

When is the last time you wrote a letter to your customers to thank them for their business and to ask how the company is treating them? People like to be given recognition, especially buyers, customers, and

in-the-trenches continual users of your company's goods and services. Try sending them a letter like this one:

> Dear _____ :
>
> I told the advertising department to hold back on any ads this
> month because I wanted to personally communicate with our
> customers to find out what you like about our product and
> how we can make it better. You have been using our products
> for nearly a year, and you have had communications with
> several different people in our company, so I would be very
> interested in your thoughts about our product, how our com-
> pany has served you, and how we might do a better job.
>
> If you wouldn't mind, I would like to call you within the week
> and speak with you about these points. If this coming week is
> inconvenient for you, please give me a call at _____ ;
> otherwise I will telephone you on _____ in
> the afternoon.
>
> Sincerely yours,
>
>
>
> Chief Executive Officer

The letter lets the customer know that he is very important to
your company. Notice the frequency of the pronoun "you" and its
juxtaposition with the pronouns "I" and "our." There is a statement
about bonding in the letter, and the fact that it comes from the CEO
raises its level of importance.

The callbacks can be divided among you and your senior marketing people. Notice the sentence in the final paragraph about the
timing of the call. Rather than simply mailing a market research
questionnaire, you and the other callback officers will ask the three
questions in the letter, either taping the calls or taking very good
notes on what you hear.

The Gift Box

Another marketing technique that has features superior to advertising is the gift box. Everyone loves to receive a gift, and just about

everyone will open a beautifully wrapped gift box. Rather than advertise next month, send a Liberty-head silver dollar minted between 1900 and 1919 to each of your customers, along with a note from the CEO saying, "We are grateful for your business."

The silver dollars may cost from $1.50 to $5.00 apiece at a coin store, and the box, wrapping paper, ribbon, labor, and postage another $2.50 per unit. If you have 500 customers, you have invested about $3,750 in gift giving. The gesture will be reciprocated with additional orders.

Why not buy additional silver dollars and mail them in gift boxes to your company's prospects? The note inside the box could say, "We look forward to doing business with you." For an extra $3,750 you can reach 500 prospects with a memorable gift that says more about the service aspects of your company than any advertisement can.

Premiums

Certain prospects and customers may be pleased to receive a silver dollar, but others will appreciate a more practical gift. A tremendous array of premiums and promotional products is displayed at the industry's annual March show in New York. There are hats, key chains, commemorative coins, notepads, pen-and-pencil sets, and more, all of which would look terrific with your company's logo on them.

Premiums remind the customer of your company, they are inexpensive, they carry a lot of information, and they are designed to be used on the customer's desk or while she is working. The Caterpillar baseball cap is widely and proudly worn by farmers and construction workers to make a statement about their skill in operating a "Cat." Your logo on a customer premium, given annually to customers and important prospects, can communicate a similar message.

Testimonial Letters

After the sale is made, the product or service installed and tested, and the bugs fixed, ask the customer for a testimonial letter. You will want to collect as many testimonial letters as possible to validate your product or service to future potential customers.

When you put together a marketing brochure, you can list the names of your clients and place a dozen testimonial letters in the brochure. These letters answer the inevitable potential customer's question: Who says your gizmo is any good?

Video News Releases

How much would you pay to have your company or its products favorably described for ninety seconds on the evening news shows in 300 major markets? Put another way, what would you pay to reach approximately 3 million serious television viewers with your message? Would you pay $35,000? That's about one cent per viewer.

Video news releases are the creation of DWJ Associates in New York City. Michael Friedman, DWJ's cofounder, realized that the local television stations were short of news stories. "So we went to advertisers and asked them to pay for DWJ to shoot a 90-second news release about their products; we would make copies and send them to about 300 stations to use as fillers." Not every station will run every video news release, but many will, often enough to bring DWJ clients such as Mobil Oil, the Tea Council, Dow Chemical, Merck, General Electric, and Durango Cookery.

At a cost of one cent per lead, if a fraction of 1% of the viewers order the product, you can find 20,000 new customers and recoup your investment quickly.

SCORECARD

Let's assume the $5 million (revenues per annum) manufacturing or service company purchases one-fourth the advertising space of the midsize ($20 million revenues) company. Using the bargaining-plus-barter strategy to reduce advertising costs, the small company turns a $125,000 annual cash flow loss into a $190,000 cash flow profit, a swing of $315,000, or 6.3% of total revenues. Not a background hymn in anybody's choir book. More like a Bible-thumping, thigh-slapping, come-to-Jesus marching song. The midsize company turns a $500,000 cash flow deficit into a $760,000 cash flow profit, a swing of $1.26 million on revenues of $20 million.

This is just for starters. And public relations, catalog testing, gifts from the CEO, premiums, and video news releases are adumbrations along the highway to the consumer that you will soon be building. They are spackle, wood filler, grout—substances that fill in the cracks not covered fully in your overall marketing strategy. In Stage Three, we discuss the implementation of marketing strategies that will take your cash flow to the moon—nonstop.

Box Score No. 5

Advertising Expenses

	$5 million sales company	*$20 million sales company*
Previous cash flow	$(125,000)	$ (500,000)
Barter deal	315,000	1,260,000
Revised cash flow	190,000	760,000
Other inexpensive substitutes for advertising	n.a.	n.a.
Total cash savings	$ 315,000	$1,260,000

Note

1. John Dewey, *Studies in Social Logic* (Chicago: University of Chicago Press, 1903).

6

Renegotiating Your Loan Costs

If your company is borrowing money from a bank or commercial finance company at interest rates higher than prime plus 4% and with your personal guarantee backstopping the loan, you are wasting money and risking your (and your family's) personal assets. However, you are far from helpless. There's a lot you can do to cut your cost of borrowing.

Insured Receivables Lending

I know that banks have gone into hiding to work off their bad loans and that small to medium-size companies have had a devil of a time finding loans since 1991. But there are lenders, and they are putting out money at prime plus 4% without requiring personal guarantees through a policy known as "insured receivables lending." It works like this.

To qualify for insured receivables lending, your company must have accounts receivable that it can pledge. The accounts receivable must be from U.S. companies rather than from individuals, government agencies, or foreign companies or government agencies. The advance rate is typically 80% of "qualified" accounts receivable, that is, those receivables that are less than 90 days old. The interest rate is prime plus 2%, or about 8.5% in the first half of 1993. The lender usually tries to tack on a few more points, or interest costs, but these can be reduced or mitigated.

In a market where receivables lenders are getting away with demanding prime plus 10% and more, in addition to requiring personal guarantees and side collateral (such as your house or savings account), why would a lender rent money at prime plus 2% and waive side collateral and personal signatures?

The answer is that, before closing on the loan, the lender asks a surety company to write a policy for the life of the loan in which the insurer agrees to pay the lender the face value of any receivable that becomes a bad debt and that the borrower cannot collect on. The surety visits the borrower and reviews the customer list and the accounts receivable aging report. It runs the names through Dun & Bradstreet, TRW, or another credit reporting agency. If it is satisfied with the collectibility of the accounts receivable, it issues a surety bond to the lender. The surety bond costs the borrower approximately 2% of the average loan balance outstanding, bringing the overall borrowing costs to prime plus 4%. But you will sleep better knowing that your personal assets are not backstopping the loan.

Because of certain audit and monitoring costs, the loan will in reality probably cost prime plus 5% in the first year, or roughly 11.5% in 1993, and thereafter, prime plus 4%, or 10.5%. If your company is paying interest of 18% per year on an average outstanding loan balance of $1 million, the savings derived from an insured receivables loan is $75,000 per year.

Other Insured Loan Programs

If domestic corporate accounts receivable are not an asset that your company is able to pledge—either because it does not generate accounts receivable or because it does but they turn very rapidly— you can pledge other assets to your lender and then locate a surety company to guarantee to the lender that if your company does not repay the loan, it will do so, typically with a 20% deductible. Insured lending on assets other than accounts receivable places greater reliance on the creditworthiness of the borrower, its cash flow, and the ready salability of the collateral if liquidation becomes necessary.

I am certain that you do not need a lesson in borrowing money, but you may need some input to focus your thinking away from the traditional and more toward the gatekeeper kind of borrowing. How does a gatekeeper borrow? By focusing on the companies and entities that will benefit from the borrower's expanded capital base. If they will truly benefit, perhaps they have something to offer the lender that has the same effect as the surety bond but saves the 2% annual fee. For instance, let's assume a supplier is unable to ship to you because you cannot pay her even though you have a customer ready, willing, and able to pay you for the goods, plus your markup. You could put the seller and the buyer together, but that would nullify your validity and eliminate your markup. To keep the two entities in the dark while effecting the purchase and sale, you need *letter-of-credit financing*. This is the oldest form of borrowing on the planet; it dates back to the origin of banking in Italy and was used to fund the merchant explorers who sold their goods and services across the seas. The letter of credit is back-to-back, from the customer to the middleman and from the middleman to the shipper, with the customer's strong credit standing in for the middleman's lack of credit. Letter-of-credit financing generally costs about prime plus one-half to prime plus 2%. It is inexpensive because the bank can hold onto the goods if it fails to get paid.

Now that you know something about letters of credit and surety bonds, you can conjure up myriad ways to borrow money at prime plus 2% to prime plus 4% without personal guarantees. How about these?

- You own a retail store with fast-turning consumer inventory sold for cash and credit cards (nonperishable). To open a second store, you want to borrow on the inventory of the first. Find a surety that will guarantee your loan for 80% of its face value if you default.
- Your region is poorly serviced by commercial airlines. You are a former pilot, and your partner was in marketing with a commercial airline. You want to open a nine-city regional commuter airline. For this you need three planes that cost $500,000 apiece, plus $500,000 in working capital, which you will raise from friends. The economies of the nine towns will benefit economically by having a regional commuter airline. Can they be persuaded to buy equipment notes from you, or will they buy the planes and lease them to you? Maybe not. If a surety took the airplanes as collateral and then guaranteed the towns' investment, then could they be persuaded to finance the airplanes? It is beginning to sound doable.

I have seen dozens of small and midsize companies borrow money from sharks at 24 to 72% interest per year, depending on the company's degree of economic soundness. Their owners and managers believe that the high interest costs are their plight, their burden. Not true. Exhibit 6-1 presents the names of the leading surety firms in the country. (Addresses and phone numbers are listed in *Best's*, available at the local library.) Give them or one of their nearby agents

Exhibit 6-1. Leading surety firms.

American Bonding Company
American International Group
American Underwriters
Avemco
Capitol Transamerica
Frontier Insurance
GAINSCO
Guaranty National
Horace Mann Educators
Integon
Markel
Navigators Group
Selective Insurance
W. R. Berkeley

a call to see if they might be interested in guaranteeing a term loan for you.

Closing Costs

Typically, lenders and lessors use preprinted agreements that have all the escape routes sealed off. This practice developed over time, as lenders and lessors were stung in the billfold and added new self-protective clauses. Many do not apply to your company, but unless you have them removed, you will pay for the costly lessons that the lenders and the lessors have learned from other customers. Before you sign the loan agreement, ask about the reasons for each clause, and negotiate away those that do not apply to you.

Ask the lender if all customers are charged a fee to close the loan. It is fairly common in secured revolving lines of credit arrangements to pay a small setup charge to the lender that covers the cost of entering your company's records and files into the lender's computer. This done, transactions can be expedited, to your benefit as well as to the lender's, as the lender receives your invoices and advances money via wire transfer to your account.

The fee also covers filing liens in the appropriate jurisdictional areas and training the lender's accounting department to process qualified accounts receivable, inventory, or equipment purchases and to disqualify the unacceptable transactions. An appropriate fee is a few thousand dollars, most of which is pure profit to the lender.

Loan Origination Fees

In unsecured transactions, there is very little reason to pay a closing cost or setup fee, so some lenders demand a *loan origination fee*. Use your most persuasive negotiating skills to remove this fee. After all, do suppliers of components charge you a fee for the privilege of being their customer? The lender or the lessor is "renting" you money, which is its primary business, and paying a fee to the lender for the privilege of becoming its customer is pushing the boundaries of reasonableness.

If the lender is adamant, you can offer the lender the opportunity to provide other services such as safe deposit, transfer agent, custodian, employee checking, or related accounts. Or you can go elsewhere.

Loan Renewal Fees

These fees can range as high as 1%, or $10,000 on a $1 million loan. The same arguments against them apply as for loan origination fees.

Loan Cancellation Fees

Some lenders charge you if your loan is prepaid by another lender before it is due. These divorce fees can reach as high as 3% of the face value of the loan. They are designed to keep you paying your existing loans even when interest rates drop and you might wish to refinance with another leader.

The divorce fee forces you to hold on to existing high-interest loans, and, if you are in a weak borrowing position, you may be stuck. If the fee is expressed as the interest the lender would have earned for the balance of the term of the loan, it can amount to tens of thousands of dollars. That is an outrageous price for doing business, but, should you leave the lender midway without paying the divorce fee, you will be in a "seeking forgiveness" rather than an "asking "permission" up-front situation, so seek counsel from both your accountant and your lawyer.

Charges for Interest Before the Loan Is Made

Under revolving lines of credit secured by accounts receivable, the lender can wire money into your account upon receipt of sales invoices, on a daily or weekly basis. If you send the invoices in on a daily basis, ask the lender if your account is credited daily. Some lenders credit weekly but charge daily, thereby increasing the interest rate. Further, if your company doesn't need the money daily, it should send its invoices in weekly. Either way, clarify this point up front.

Interest Rate Adjustments

Many lenders tie their interest rates to the prime rate. When the prime rate changes, your cost of money changes. But when is the adjustment made? If you think interest rates are going to rise, ask for a monthly adjustment. If you think they will fall, ask for a daily adjustment. The cost savings can be significant.

For example, assume that your company has an outstanding loan of $500,000 at a prime of 10% plus 2 or 3 points. If the loan remains outstanding for one year and the prime rate does not change, your company will pay $65,000 in interest. If the prime rate is reduced .5 percent on the fifth day of the month, your savings for the month will be $208 if the adjustment is made immediately, rather than at the end of the month.

Recourse vs. Nonrecourse Loans

The loan agreement may say that in the event of nonpayment of the loan, "the lender has full recourse against the company." This language occurs frequently in secured loans. It means that if the lender cannot recover its loan from the assets that are providing collateral, it can make its claim against the company. That is known as belt-and-suspenders borrowing. Secured loans are expensive, but the lender is supposed to know how to convert its collateral to cash if it needs to. Recourse lending gives the lender a second chance to clean you out. In a word: Avoid recourse loans, and insist on nonrecourse.

Extra Bank Benefits

Ask your lender what benefits your company can obtain as a result of becoming its customer. How about free checking accounts for employees? Or treating deposits as "good funds" on the day of deposit? Check-cashing privileges for employees is yet another benefit. Free company credit cards (if they are needed) might be another. Note that there are many "affinity" credit card offerings that offer the user frequent flyer points when the card is used to make purchases. If your company uses affinity credit cards, determine in advance how the frequent flyer points will be used. Perhaps they can be awarded to the employee who offers the best cost-savings suggestion of the year.

Treating Your Banker Fairly

Provide financial information to your banker on a regular basis. Avoid hitting her with unpleasant surprises by calling her in advance of a negative earnings report and asking for an appointment to explain the problem and your solution to it. Be sure to send your banker the accountant's management letter along with the year-end audit.

Maintain positive balances in at least one account. Use other services to enable the bank to earn fees. These services might include a safe deposit account, one or more personal accounts, trust accounts, and transfer agent services. Introduce new accounts and new loan opportunities to the bank.

If your company receives a windfall deposit, such as from a large private placement, let the money sit at the bank for a few days interest-free so that the bank can earn a few thousand dollars on it. Then, when you negotiate interest rates in the future, you can point to the various ways you have helped the bank to earn fees through your relationship.

SCORECARD

To calculate how much cash you can save and how much cash flow you can generate by shrewder, tougher scrutiny of loan documents and by using a surety bond to ensure repayment to the lender, assume that the $5 million (revenues) company has $1 million in average loans outstanding and the $20 million (revenues) company has $3 million in borrowings. Here are the possible savings:

Box Score No. 6

Savings on Loan Costs

	Small company	Midsize comany
Interest rate	$60,000	$180,000
Origination fee	10,000	20,000
Renewal fee	5,000	15,000
Audit fee	5,000	10,000
Total savings	$80,000	$225,000

7

Are Your Accounting Costs Too High?

There is no question in my mind that your accounting fees are too high. Accounting firms are similar to law firms in that they like to multiple-bill their clients. Rather than assign one person to your audit or accounting needs, they generally assign a partner, a senior associate, and a wet-behind-the-ears new recruit. You are training the junior associate and paying the accounting firm for the privilege. You may be training the senior associate, as well. Some accounting firms bring in a fourth and a fifth associate with specialized skills in taxes, pension planning, health care, and other areas. It is time to take the accounting cost problem in hand and cut your expenses in this area in half. There are several ways to go about this. But you begin with the all-purpose word: *ask*.

First, evaluate your audit needs. Are you a franchising company? Do you have several joint ventures or partnerships? Do you export? Are you planning to go public? Then ask other accounting firms to bid on your work. In each instance, you will want to identify a specialist within the accounting firm who is familiar with your kind of business. Accountants at small firms in many cases will have to learn at your expense, whereas the larger firms will provide creative accounting solutions—read enhanced profits and reduced taxes—in areas that are often complicated and confusing to the novice.

Large accounting firms usually offer small-company prices to attract new business. Most of their new clients come from the entrepreneurial community, and the price of the first year's audit, assuming nothing extraordinary is required, will generally meet the bid that you receive from a smaller firm that lacks your specialty.

Accounting Charges

Here are some questions to ask your company's accounting firm in order to lower its audit fees:

- ☐ What is the price of this year's audit?
- ☐ Does it include the tax filings?
- ☐ Who is assigned to it?
- ☐ What are their billing rates?
- ☐ Are they experienced in this kind of business?
- ☐ Does the audit price include the management letter?
- ☐ What work can we do on the books internally to lower the audit cost?
- ☐ Does the cost include the defense of your work in the event of an IRS audit or litigation?

Let's look at what is behind these questions. Accounting firms sell their time. They hire intelligent young people, train them, and mark up their cost two to five times. Let's assume that one junior accountant, one senior accountant, and one partner are assigned to perform your company's audit, that they earn $40,000, $60,000 and $125,000 per annum, respectively, and that they each work 2,500 hours each year. Their "raw material" costs are thus $16 per hour, $24 per hour, and $50 per hour, respectively.

For the accounting firm to bid your job intelligently, it must estimate the number of hours the job will take. At the preaudit meeting, ask for that estimate. That will give you a pretty fair idea of the markup factor, which will help you negotiate the fee. For example, assume the accounting firm bids $40,000 and estimates 100 hours, or $400 per hour. If you divide the 100 hours among the three auditors and compare the costs actually incurred by the firm, you will probably conclude that you are being bid high. (See Exhibit 7-1.)

Exhibit 7-1. Computation of accounting costs.

	Accounting Firm's Actual Cost
33 × junior accountant × $16 =	$ 528
33 × senior accountant × $24 =	792
34 × partner × $50 =	1,700
100 hours	$3,020

Rather than taking a 500% markup, the accounting firm is trying to achieve a 3,300% markup. You have room to negotiate all the way down to $16,000 and still give them their 500% markup.

Pricing for Special Services

Audit work for initial public offerings (IPOs) is very lucrative because it requires many more hours than does a plain vanilla audit. When a computer chain that I had invested in went public in 1984, the audit fee for the fiscal year end and for the "stub period" between the end of the fiscal year and the issuance of the prospectus was approximately $250,000, or roughly 10% of the company's revenues. (The stub period audit is required by the Securities and Exchange Commission. The audited financial statement in a new-issue prospectus must be not more than 135 days old.)

In this case, the accounting firm had to await the successful outcome of the IPO before it could receive most of its fee. This no doubt caused uneasiness among its senior partners. If the IPO had failed to come off, would any of the computer company's liabilities, including the audit fee, be paid?

To avoid misunderstandings on special jobs, set the terms beforehand. "If the IPO succeeds," you might suggest to the partner in charge of your account, "we will pay you $25,000 up front and $125,000 out of the proceeds. But if the IPO fails, we would like to have 12 months to retire the back-end at 10% interest." In this manner, the accounting firm can do its work with objectivity, knowing it will be paid no matter what.

Sue the Accountant

Stockholders who have lost money investing in venture capital and acquisition funds and who have had money in savings and loans and commercial banks that have failed have hired piranhas in pin-striped suits to attempt to recover their investment. The piranhas are trained to go for the deep pocket, which in a busted deal is surely not the banks' officers (unless there was fraud). So they go after the accountants and the wealthy directors, if there are any. The partners of the accounting firms are covered to some extent by D&O insurance, but the increasing frequency of this kind of suit has made the D&O carriers squeamish, and they have raised rates and reduced coverage to accounting firms.

But don't fill the floor with tears for the accountants. They are revenue-driven—"Fill those hours, people, that's all we've got to sell," as the senior partner of one of the largest accounting firms was known to yell at his troops. Conflicts of interest are not uncommon; accounting firms all too frequently agree to audit companies that borrow money from banks that are long-standing audit clients and raise capital from insurance companies and funds that are also clients. Although, before you sign its engagement letter, the accounting firm will give you a statement to read that has a section on litigation, in which the firm states that it will defend its work for you if your company is sued on the numbers. You can take that message with a grain of salt. If the company that sues you is an audit client of your accounting firm of longer standing and of higher annual fees, the accounting firm will abandon you as if you were the Titanic.

An accounting firm's signature on your audit is not the guarantee it used to be. Accounting firms are like the Marines landing on Iwo Jima: They fire their shots (send their employees) in all directions, and whenever they get a hit (find a large fee-paying client), they run in that direction. If this means losing face with smaller clients, too bad.

What does this mean? It means when you hire an accounting firm, have it sign an engagement letter that includes this statement: "In the event that the Company, and/or its senior management, and/or its directors are sued because of alleged misstatements, false statements, or fraudulent statements concerning the financial statements, tax returns, and footnotes related thereto, our firm will defend those financial statements, tax returns, and footnotes to the best of our ability at no cost to the Company."

The Engagement Letter

Many companies hire auditors and accountants without an *engagement letter*, which is a fancy expression for "contract." That is not wise because you then have an open-ended arrangement in which the fee can go sky-high even though the work product may be unacceptable; the accountants can bolt and run if one of their clients sues your company or you; and you can spend years in court trying to determine who said what about the services the accounting firm was supposed to perform.

To avoid an open-ended fee arrangement, ask the accounting firm you have selected to submit an engagement letter specifying the scope of the assignment and its cost. The letter should state the amount of the retainer, if there is one, the number of hours, the people assigned to the task, and their rates. The letter should further specify that the audit will include a management letter.

A partner of the firm should sign the letter, and the chief executive officer of your company should countersign it.

The Management Letter

The management letter is a memorandum from the accounting firm to your company telling you what you did right, what you did wrong, and where you could stand some improvement in your bookkeeping, accounting, and financial controls. The memorandum is generally written by the partner or senior associate assigned to your account and signed by a partner. Accounting firms frequently don't offer to do a management letter because it requires extra effort on their part, but I suggest that you always ask for one to be included with the annual audit.

The reasons you need the management letter are several: (1) you honestly want to know where you could improve in the area of financial controls and bookkeeping, (2) you want to sit down with the accountants to discuss the letter, using the letter as the basis for exploring new data-processing and data-collection systems, staff strengths and weaknesses, and ways to improve the accounting functions, and (3) in the event you are sued by a client of the accounting firm, at least you will have the accounting firm's letter to take into court to show the judge that the firm (ostensibly) approved of your recordkeeping.

Handling Suspect Information

When you are suspicious of a transaction someone in your firm has entered into, do not withhold it from your auditor. For example, if your firm paid a finder's fee to a third party to close an important sale, disclose the fee to your auditor and explain that it was a cost of doing business. The auditor may treat it as a selling cost or a discount. If the finder's fee was paid as a bribe to an employee of that company that purchased your product, disclose that as well and be prepared for some serious consequences, such as termination of the briber, exposure of the bribee, and the need to come clean with regulatory agencies, stockholders, and others to whom full disclosure is required.

Large accounting firms have seen just about every curious trans-action a business can conceive. Full disclosure up front and a willing-ness to correct the problem will bond the accounting firm to your company, and its creative staff will assist you in ferreting out the problem and eliminating it in the future.

SCORECARD

The objective of this chapter is to help you focus on making certain demands from your company's accounting firm that will benefit the company now and in the future. Chief among these demands is a signed engagement letter with an audit fee reduction. The second most important demand is the management letter. The third is clarity about special jobs, such as the work involved in preacquisition, due diligence, and going public. If these three demands are made, then you will be able to lower and control your accounting costs while improving the quality of the service.

Let's assume that the accounting fee charged the small company has been $20,000 per year and that charged the midsize company has been $50,000 per year. The cash savings in fee reductions are esti-mated to be $2,000 for the small company and $5,000 for the midsize company per annum.

Box Score No. 7

Saving on Accounting Expenses

	$5 million sales company	$20 million sales company
Savings resulting from:		
• Competitive bidding	$1,000	$2,000
• Doing more audit prep work in-house	1,000	2,000
• Eliminating multiple accounting firm partners at meetings	—	1,000
Total savings	$2,000	$5,000

8

Cutting Back on Travel Costs

Resourceful fliers have several ways to minimize the cost of flying these days. They can buy tickets from travel agents who work with consolidators, or they can purchase tickets through agents known as "rebaters," such as Travel Avenue in Chicago, which provides a 7% cash rebate (minus a $10 service fee) on each ticket sold. Another possible source of reduced-fare tickets are the new fee-based travel clubs, like Pace Warehouse Travel Club, which offer similar rebates.

The price incentives represent the airlines' efforts to reconcile contradictory problems. Carriers suffer from both excess capacity and insufficient revenue resulting from low fares. So they release a modest number of steeply discounted tickets in order to fill the extra seats but disguise the distribution channels in order to conceal the tickets' availability from most customers.

When airlines sell tickets through consolidators, they aren't exactly giving away their product. The industry puts heavy restrictions and penalties on the reduced fares. Customers typically can't use the tickets for mileage credits on their frequent-flyer accounts. They also can't exchange the tickets or get upgrades or refunds. Even special meals are restricted. Frequently, the rebater or consolidator deals in cash or checks to avoid credit-card charges. To compensate for these conditions, the wholesaler offers dramatic savings, as demonstrated in Exhibit 8-1.

Airlines' published fares are unrestricted round-trip coach tickets. The special fares are offered through wholesale distributors and can be purchased at some travel agencies. They do not require advance purchases or Saturday night stays, but many restrictions apply. Special-fare domestic tickets require a minimum two-night stay.

Exhibit 8-1. Discount air fares vs. published rates.

Route	Published Rate	Special Fare	Airline
Seattle-New York	$1,300	$480	TWA
Portland-Houston	1,180	425	TWA
New York-Los Angeles	1,600	400	N/A
Boston-Miami	1,000	460	N/A
New York-London	2,084	470	All majors
San Francisco-Hong Kong	1,055	780	All majors
Chicago-Paris	2,336	600	All majors

Source: *The Wall Street Journal*, March 12, 1993, p. B-1.

If you make a reservation 21 days or more in advance of the flight date, most domestic and some foreign airlines will offer you a 25% discount off standard coach fare. Assuming the standard cost of the flight is $450 one way, the savings is $112.50, bringing the ticket price to $337.50. The catch is that if you change the time or day or carrier for that particular ticket, the airline will ask you to pay back the $112.50.

I polled a handful of frequent business flyers, and they explained to me how they never lose the $112.50 when they change the time or day of the flight or change the carrier (but still fly to the same destination). There are three tactics. The first is to take advantage of a little-known technical loophole known as Rule 240; the second is borrowed from the Cuban missile crisis; and the third is known as the "Speedy Gonzalez tactic."

The Rule 240 Loophole

Hidden in the fine print of all U.S. airlines' domestic fare guidelines is the little-known Rule 240, which permits airline service counter personnel, largely at their own discretion, to reroute a passenger on a competing airline *at no additonal cost* when the traveler's plans are interrupted. The airline employee can invoke Rule 240 and save you the 25% if he or she feels like doing it, even if the airline is not at fault for the travel interruption.

The rule is almost always invoked in the traveler's favor if the traveler misses the flight for one of the following reasons:

- The flight is overbooked or canceled.
- The airline substitutes a smaller plane that cannot accommodate everyone.
- Your connecting flight was late in arriving.

Even if none of these has occurred, sympathetic airline service counter employees may rebook you on a competitor's flight if you can persuade them that the seat assigned you is unacceptable or that you and your travel partner need to sit together but the seat assignment on the ticketed flight do not permit it.

The key to persuading the ticket agent is to mention Rule 240. But remember to cite the rule politely. Make certain that an alternative flight will get to the destination before your ticketed flight. Name the alternative flight, and provide the employee with the flight number and departure time. Never demand the change of tickets—that will lead to a swift and firm turndown.

The Cuban Missile Crisis Strategy

As you may recall, President John F. Kennedy employed a risky but effective strategy in 1962, when he forced the Soviets to remove their missiles from Cuba. First, Kennedy notified General Secretary Nikita Khrushchev of the Soviet Union that if that country did not remove its missiles by a certain date, he would send a significant portion of the U.S. Navy to knock them out. In response, Khrushchev sent a cable to Kennedy refusing to honor the demand. Kennedy then pretended he had never received the Soviet leader's cable and sent the navy to blockade Cuba. The Soviets knuckled under, packed up their missiles, and pulled them out of Cuba. This strategy has been used in diplomacy and business very selectively for many years, but Kennedy is given credit for it.

Now, on to the airline counter, where we're trying to save $112.50. To deploy this strategy, you arrive at the check-in counter 25 minutes before the flight for which you already have a reservation. You say you wish to change your ticket. A line of 20 to 30 nervous business travelers, students, and noisy families forms behind you. They are your navy. The airline counter person is Khrushchev.

The counter attendant asks you how you would like to pay for the $112.50 additional charge. You profess ignorance of any additional charge. The attendant explains that this particular ticket cannot be changed without paying a 25% penalty. You say you were not informed of this and that it's news to you.

The counter attendant is mildly impressed when you pull out your frequent flyer card for his or her airline, which suggests that you are a preferred customer. But it is your stoicism that encourages the counter attendant to call the manager out from the back room. Do not shift your stance during this brief pause, or your navy might take that as a signal that your resolve is slipping.

When the manager comes out to the counter, the first thing that he or she sees is more than 20 concerned people lined up behind a single serious-looking business traveler. If the manager checks the time, you're halfway home because there are more than 20 passengers who have to get down to the gate and onto the airplane in 15 minutes. You have a 50-50 chance of persuading the manager that the penalty is news to you. A manager who has heard this story before will insist that you step aside while the other passengers move ahead. You don't have to move—Kennedy didn't move when Khrushchev sent that cable. If you move, you lose. Winning is having the manager punch in a new ticket without collecting the additional fare.

Most business travelers do not have 20 minutes to spend on this game, the outcome of which cannot be guaranteed. Thus, you may want to try the absolute sure technique: the Speedy Gonzalez tactic.

The Speedy Gonzalez Tactic

As with many things, the simplest tactic is the best. The Speedy Gonzalez tactic involves running up to the service desk at the departure gate just as the door is closing on the flight you wish to take. The service manager will take your ticket and say, "Hurry on board. We're taking off" as he or she closes the door behind you. You need say nothing at all.

This often happens to business travelers who have been standing at the pay phone across from the service counter with one eye on the attendant and one eye on your list of calls to return. They feel that they cannot lose a minute of marketing or receivables collection time. They have squeezed cash out of airport waiting time and saved 25% of the price of the ticket.

SCORECARD

Because it is small and pays attention to details such as discounts on travel costs, my firm has achieved a savings of 18.3% on travel costs. If your company is larger and has a greater number of travelers, then you have more leverage with airline carriers, hotels, and car rental companies. If you are bartering as a means of lowering advertising costs, then you can select from among an excess of airline seats, hotel beds, and car rentals.

It is possible to slash 50% off your travel costs by purchasing airline tickets through consolidators, obtaining hotel and rental car discounts through associations and affinity groups, and watching carefully for frequent flyer and similar deals. The $5 million (sales) company is likely to have salespersons who travel once a week at a cost to the company of $1,000 per week, or $50,000 per year. The $20 million (sales) company is likely to spend three to four times that amount on travel. The savings—available for the asking—are estimated as follows:

Box Score No. 8

Travel Expense Saving

	$5 million sales company	$20 million sales company
Travel costs:		
Airplane tickets	$30,000	$120,000
Hotel rooms	12,500	50,000
Rental cars	7,500	30,000
Total	$50,000	$200,000
Savings at 36%	$18,000	$ 72,000

9

Going Nose-to-Nose With Your Suppliers

A manufacturer of fax modems recently hired my firm to assist in developing a workout plan and in raising venture capital. A supplier of microchips had shipped it a large quantity of bad product, and it had to remanufacture three months' worth of shipments and to fight an onslaught of customer complaints. While doing this, the company's accounts payable ballooned from $500,000 to $1.5 million, and the over-90-day payables swelled to $485,000.

The company's chief executive officer had never faced a crisis of this magnitude. Every day the mail brought certified demand letters from lawyers threatening the company with instant extinction if it did not pay the lawyers' clients. His suppliers were threatening to cut him off if the company did not pay their invoices immediately.

It will not surprise you that they were all bluffing. Lucy says harsher things to Charlie Brown in the "Peanuts" cartoon strip—and she means them—than collection lawyers say to slow-paying customers.

We made the important vendors an offer—if they would keep shipping parts, the company would pay C.O.D. for every shipment received, with the understanding that the payments would be applied to the oldest invoices first. In this way the company would work down its oldest invoices.

We negotiated this deal with 25 suppliers. Twenty-three accepted it, and two asked for $1.50 for each $1.00 of new invoices to be paid C.O.D. Think about that for a moment. Only two of the vendors knew how to seize the opportunity to leverage the fax modem manufacturer into paying down its debt. The others were happy being stuffees.

Suppliers are incredibly cooperative. You want a favor from them? Just ask. Wal-Mart Stores has been doing it masterfully for over a decade. "But they have clout," you argue. You have clout, also. You are a customer, and customers are a very precious commodity. Your suppliers want to keep you; just consider the relatively deep discounts that trade creditors are willing to accept in Chapter 11 reorganizations. The percentage recovery by trade creditors was less than 40% in 1991, according to a study by the U.S. bankruptcy court system, compared with 60 cents on the dollar in 1980. The reason is generally considered to be the rise in the number of business failures, which tends to make customers who have the money to pay more valuable. Stated more simply, it's a buyer's market.

If you don't ask for something, you will never know if you could have gotten it. Asking is the basis of entrepreneurship. It is fundamental to launching a business on customer financing, such as direct mail operations, franchises, party plans, and all the wonderful subscription-based and membership-based businesses, such as The Price Club, Book-of-the-Month Club, and Mary Kay Cosmetics. Without asking for payment up front, three-fourths of the businesses in the United States that have been started by women would not exist, because women tend to start businesses based on customer trust and customer financing, there being a paucity of venturesome capital willing to follow women entrepreneurs.

I suggest that you ask your suppliers one or more of the following questions:

- Are you giving my company the best discount you possibly can?
- Is there any customer that is getting a better discount than you are giving to my company?
- Do you have any affinity programs that you have not mentioned to us—frequent flyer points, free cellular telephones, travel discounts?
- Are we paying you on average faster than your other customers? If we are, we want recognition for that—a discount of 2%. Or we want to pay you two weeks slower, whichever you prefer.

If you don't ask your suppliers these questions, you will never know if they would have cooperated. Many of them would have, because they have bonded with you. They have probably discounted your obligation to pay with their lender, and you are important to their ability to borrow. Thus, as a customer, you have more leverage than you possibly thought.

Negotiating With Office Equipment Suppliers

Just about every office equipment supplier is in a slugfest with every other supplier to sell copiers, fax machines, telephone systems, and personal computers. American industry has incredible negotiating power with these companies. If it is time for your company to upgrade or replace some office equipment, you are in the driver's seat. Providers of office equipment are competing feverishly to win your order. Here's an example.

My company recently bought a top-of-the-line photocopier priced at about $30,000. That was list price.

I said to the salesman, "That's list price. How much will you give us for our copier in a trade-in?" (I knew it was on its last legs.) He offered $5,000.

I accepted because that was five times more than it was worth; further, it was costing us $600 every month to repair it.

I then asked, "Okay. This is the 1990s. What are your affinity deals?"

Without blinking, the salesman said, "If you switch from your overnight courier to the one we have a deal with, an overnight letter will cost you $8.00 rather than $9.00."

I took it.

With unaccustomed glee in winning concessions from a major office equipment dealer, I called my friend Arnold, senior partner in a medium-size law firm.

I told Arnold about my deal.

He responded, "So what? I switched our long-distance service from AT&T to Sprint, and they gave us a Canon 900 copier for free."

You can't win 'em all.

The Advent of Just-in-Time, Customer-Driven Selling

Whether your sales are $3.5 million or $350 million per year, the principal driver of how much you order from your suppliers, what you order, and how much you pay is your customers' purchases. And the principal means of gathering and measuring that information is a chip inside your personal computer. The savings to you is enormous; for one thing, you can begin to eliminate the wholesaler, reaping a savings of 20% to 25% of retail selling price.

Thanks to the semiconductor, several brilliantly managed retail chains, including Wal-Mart, Stein Mart, and The Limited, are structured around information from the sales floor. Whenever a customer buys a product, the information goes directly—in "real time"—to the manufacturer's plant, where it is automatically converted into a manufacturing schedule and into delivery instructions: when to ship, how to ship, where to ship. This system largely eliminates the 25% of the retail price that used to go toward getting merchandise from the manufacturer's loading dock to the retailer's store. As a result, the chains can undersell local competitors despite their generally higher labor costs.

If you run a chain of retail stores, the key to lowering costs and passing the savings on to customers is integrating customer purchases with manufacturing schedules in order to create a just-in-time delivery system. The bar-code reader is the key to capturing information at the checkout counter and relaying it to manufacturers through telecommunications networks. As some of the greater retailers have it: Retail is in the detail.

Prior to the availability of real-time information capturing and handling, day-to-day operating decisions had to be manufacturing decisions, driven by plant and production schedules, capacity, and costs. Now that you know in milliseconds what goes on at every checkout counter in your system, purchase decisions can be based on what the customers are buying and not buying and controlled by the people who have the information—retailers and distributors. Increasingly, retailers and distributors are achieving gatekeeper power over manufacturers. Suppliers have to restructure their plants for flexible manufacturing, or production organized around the flow of market information, rather than around the flow of materials as in traditional manufacturing. If your company manufactures a product line that is sold through retail chains and if you become linked to the chains' customers' buying habits, you will be able to eliminate many layers of management. Further, when entire markets become organized around external information captured at the checkout counter, far fewer intermediaries are needed. Wholesalers and warehouses will become obsolete. Supermarket chains will order direct from the producers for direct shipment to their stores. Banks will be reduced in number and in size because many of them finance the wholesale inventory stocking functions, which will be things of the past.

Leveraging Your Suppliers

If your company is capturing information at the point of purchase, or if it has the means to, then you are in a position to exercise considerable leverage over your suppliers. If you have multiple sources of supply for raw materials and other components, you can make demands regarding price and delivery schedules that you would not previously have believed possible. You can literally demand 25% reductions in price, just-in-time deliveries, and payment periods of 60 days, rather than 30 or 45 days. Some suppliers may balk. But there will always be at least one that will want your business. Why? Because you can persuade that one supplier that it does not need a salesperson to call on you, a middle manager to oversee your account, or a lot of warehouse space to store your goods. If you share your cost-saving ideas with suppliers for every key component, you can convince them that they will be just as profitable even if they ship your product at 25% below last year's prices.

Installing the System

To make an on-line, real-time checkout-counter-to-source-of-supply system work, you will have to invest some money. Think of a model trains set with information as the railroad cars, fiber optic telephone lines (or, eventually, cable TV) as the railroad track, your office as the switching system, your checkout counters (or, if you are the supplier, your customers' checkout counters) as the loading platforms, and your suppliers' offices as the unloading platforms.

You will have to establish guidelines similar to the following with your suppliers:

- You are to maintain a minimum of 30 units of each of the 10 SKUs we buy from you at each of our 25 stores.
- When the in-stock quantity falls to 30, immediately ship 15 units to that store, adjusted for the sales level this month last year (or any other seasonal weighing factor).
- Fax a copy of the shipping order to our central (or regional buying office), and we will sign it and fax it back to give you a confirmed purchase order.
- Fax the signed purchase order to the destination store with the time that you plan to deliver the order in the next 24 to 48 hours.
- We will pay you in 30 days, but at 15% less than we paid for the same SKUs last year before we put you on line, real time, to our cash registers.

Why should your suppliers accept a 15% cut in price? Because they will turn their volume more quickly. Because you are going to kill the competition with your lower prices, and your growth will mean more sales for the supplier. Because the supplier will save money on warehouse space and production costs. Because the supplier will be able to lay off five middle managers who used to supervise shipping, warehouse, construction operations, and production. And because the supplier will be able to reduce its borrowing costs.

SCORECARD

The savings from implementing an on-line, real-time inventory management system will eventually be as much as a 7.5% reduction in Cost of Goods Sold, assuming that you are able to install an "information unloading dock" in the offices of one-half of your suppliers.

For the $5 million (revenues) manufacturer, the ultimate savings will be on the order of $200,000 to $250,000 per annum. For the $20 million (revenues) distributor, the savings will be in the range of $1 million to $1.25 million per annum. These are long-term benefits with enormous cash-flow-generating potential. To achieve them will require an up-front investment in personal computers, data-handling and data-processing software, and a well-planned telecommunications system.

Count on financing these changes with the cash generated from ideas in the other chapters of this book. This is one moving train you do not want to miss.

10

Rethinking Your Employee Needs

Layered management teams are necessary in an information-based economy. There are fewer steps in the ordering process and fewer warehouses to open, staff, stock, and operate. Products can come directly from the manufacturer to the retailer in quantities based on cash register transactions. With fewer goods in storage, there is less inventory to finance and a concomitant reduction in the need for people in your finance department. It may be possible to shrink the number of people in your data-processing department once the information system is running and employees have desktop and laptop computers and can order downloads from the central processor.

Employee Leasing

An extreme measure that some companies are using to slash payroll costs is employee leasing. The argument in its favor can be compelling.

When was the last time somebody made you this offer: I will take all of your employees on my payroll and rent them back to you. They will receive substantially improved health benefits, and when you want to terminate them, I will find them another job. You can save the payroll costs of your human resources department—at least $20,000 per person. I will fill out all the government and insurance forms for the employees and handle all terminations, and you will enjoy extra time for other management tasks.

Tempting? That's the offer employee leasing companies make, and by the early 1990s, 20,000 U.S. companies had taken them up on it.

Employee leasing companies make money by charging their clients the sum of payroll plus benefits plus a fee. They make an additional profit by negotiating substantially less expensive benefits packages for their employees. However, the fee charged to clients is small in comparison with the savings in management time and employee hassles.

Following are the services that employee leasing companies provide for your people:

- Processing payroll checks
- Providing you with weekly payroll and billing reports
- Filing and paying all state and federal employer taxes
- Preparing W-2 forms at year-end for all employees
- Providing a comprehensive employee health insurance program
- Processing Section 125 benefits deductions
- Processing all insurance claims
- Offering and administering COBRA (Comprehensive Omnibus Benefits Retirement Act) benefits
- Providing coverage for workers' compensation, issuing certificates, and administering claims
- Administering state employment claims
- Providing a credit union
- Providing an in-house human resources consultant
- Providing in-house legal counsel

GTE, Holiday Corporation, Greyhound, Hospital Corporation of America, and thousands of other companies are leasing some or all of their employees from the 400 employee leasing companies in the United States. The average size of companies leasing their employees is 30 people, and many of them are rapidly expanding companies whose managers are too busy steering their companies' growth to pay the necessary attention to government and insurance compliance forms.

Virginia Munichman, co-owner of Mini-City Dry Cleaners & Laundromat in Raleigh, North Carolina, leases her 24-person staff. "I value not having to worry about taking care of taxes, employees' hours, and issuing checks." she says.

Walt Dixon, president of Wal-Tech, a yarn-dye facility for woven fabrics that has 250 workers in three plants in three states, compared employee leasing with the services of a payroll firm and chose employee leasing. He told the *Triangle Business* newsweekly that the amount of time he saves on office work is immense. He said he'd spent 25 years dealing with things such as people and payroll, and now recognizes the value of a package that leaves him not having to deal with life insurance agents or tax people.

Insurance companies are also fans of employee leasing, for two reasons. First, it allows them to bill one company (the leasing company) for their services, rather than several hundred, and they can monitor the insurance records with far fewer auditors. Second, it takes fewer salespeople to call on 400 employee leasing companies than it does to serve the nearly 20,000 companies in the United States that now lease their employees.

Is Employee Leasing Cost-Effective?

Leasing offers two primary savings: it eliminates the salaries and related costs of a human resources department and it offers a huge savings in management time. Gary Stouffer, president and co-owner of Modumed of Westlake Village, California, eliminated a $20,000-per-year personnel administration position. Stouffer claims, "I'm saving money by leasing my employees."

Marvin R. Selter, chairman of National Staff Network, the nation's largest employee leasing company, with approximately 35,000 employees, says that its typical client had been spending about 28% of its revenues on payroll, benefits, and employee administration costs; now the typical client spends 22% on employee leasing.

The Benefits to Workers

There are three big advantages of employee leasing for workers: (1) no layoffs, (2) improved medical benefits, and (3) access to credit unions.

1. *No Layoffs.* Employee leasing companies continually network with their clients. They know who needs staffing, in what positions, at what rate, and when. Should a client terminate a handful of people, the employee leasing company can usually find them new jobs immediately. Not only does that please the employee, but it reduces the potential for litigation.

2. *Improved Medical Benefits.* Most employee leasing companies offer a comprehensive package of health care benefits, including medical and dental coverage, prescription reimbursement, vision care, and life insurance, that would be the envy of any auto worker. One employee leasing company provides such a package for its

employees for $78 per person per month. Of this amount, the health insurance plan costs the employee leasing company $64 per month.

3. *Access to Credit Unions.* Many companies that choose the employee leasing option are fairly small and do not have employee credit unions, private banks that provide their members with low-interest mortgages, car loans, credit cards, and personal loans. With tens of thousands of members, employee leasing companies can staff and operate credit unions for hundreds of 25-person companies.

The Growth of Employee Leasing

Half of the employees under lease in the United States are in the states, including New York, California, Ohio, and Pennsylvania, that have historically been labor pressure cookers, as evidenced by their high tax rates, history of bitter strikes, and high incidence of wrongful termination disputes. Employees need a few breaks, and employee leasing gives them more benefits than even the shrewdest labor negotiator has ever dared demand. Surely, there is good reason for the prediction by management guru Peter Drucker and other economic soothsayers that more than 10 million workers will be under contract to employee leasing companies by the mid 1990s.

Reducing Your Administrative Staff

Another way to cut your payroll costs is to spin off your administrative personnel into independent contractor organizations that perform necessary services for your company, as well as for others. The data-processing department is a prime candidate for a spin-off. You might also consider putting the advertising, sales, and receivables collection departments on retainer contracts that include success fees. You will immediately save on their health insurance costs while they—being in small companies—will be able to buy low-cost and potentially profitable association-based health insurance.

Reducing Salaries

Across-the-board salary reductions are a mandatory first step for all personnel before you consider layoffs. The biggest cuts should be made in the largest salaries. Salary cuts for key people should be discussed one-on-one, rather than being announced in an impersonal form letter. Some people may be in the most expensive years in their working lives, with children in college, while others may be in less expensive years. Some may be able to endure 20% cuts, while for others a 10% cut may be the maximum endurable.

Cuts at the production-worker level cannot be handled in an impersonal way, because production workers tend to feel, and rightly so in most instances, that they are, like mushrooms, kept in the dark. A tactic I have found useful is to go into the factory for a shirts-sleeve meeting with the head of production, explaining the situation and requesting everyone's extra effort. In one case, the head of production and I fielded workers' questions for an hour and then asked for a voluntary 15% pay cut. A few hands were raised at first. Then, when all hands were up, we pulled out a wad of crisp fifty-dollar bills and passed them around to everyone. "You see," the head of production said, "we're going to pull through these dark days if we all pull together."

We routinely passed out fifty-dollar bills whenever the production workers came in on Saturdays or did an exceptional job at getting out an order without flaws or providing warranty and repair work in record time. I also recommended in this case spreading shares of the company's stock around to all employees to compensate for longer hours and lower pay.

Changing Your Relationship With Your Sales Staff

If you are currently paying your salespersons a base or a salary plus commissions, then you are being inversely leveraged. You are being tollgated by them, which is not the way it should be since you developed the product, produced the product, and raised the capital to get the product to market. They should consider themselves privileged to have the opportunity to sell your product, and if they do a good job you will compensate them appropriately.

Let me explain myself. Although I don't want you to throw the book in the trash because I am telling you to cut your sales team's salaries to zero and make them pay their own expenses, that is in fact what I am suggesting.

You will be opening from 10 to 25 new marketing channels, so your primary channel—feet on the street—will no longer be the primary source of your company's cash flow. Many of these new channels will pump in cash flow up-front, without requiring the expense of building and training a sales staff. At least five of the new marketing channels in combination may well outperform your sales team.

Your typical salesperson is given a product, a territory, some initial training, some marketing materials, and a high commission—at least 20%—and that is all. Now you are going to take away the base or salary and the expense advance and transform him from an employee into an independent contractor, hired to sell your product, as well as other, noncompeting products. In return, you will compensate the salesperson with a commission based on (1) the dollar value of his sales, (2) the gross profit margin of his sales, (3) the renewal of his sales the next year, and (4) the number of people he hires and trains to sell your product in subregions within his market. The recruits, in turn, will be compensated the same way; that is, they will be encouraged to hire and train recruits to sell in sub-submarkets. The map of the territory in which you sell must be drawn carefully to keep the playing field level, and no salesperson or recruit should be required to purchase products in advance, which is one of the negatives in multilevel marketing scams.

By compensating everyone in sales for *selling, hiring,* and *training,* you reward them for selling or teaching—pushing product or pushing information—which most salespersons can do. You remove from them the responsibilities of prospecting. You will do their lead generating for them, through bouncebacks and telemarketing, and they will pay you for leads in their zip codes.

Moreover, you will remove the sales department from your payroll and thereby save the enormous costs of managing them, paying their insurance, withholding their taxes, and working out their personnel problems. If your sales force become independent contractors, these issues will no longer be your problem.

If you untether your sales department and work cooperatively with a team of independent contractors, the sales team will suffer economically and leave you willingly if they fail to perform. No wrongful termination suits. No whining for more advertising support. The Law of Reciprocity prevails.

Involuntary Terminations: Where to Cut

My feelings about terminations without specific causes are that they should be avoided at all costs, with spin-offs and salary reductions tried first. However, if layoffs are unavoidable, they need to be carefully thought out.

In finance and administration, you need at a minimum an accounts receivable clerk, an accounts payable clerk, a bookkeeper or controller, and a human resources officer. If you are two or more people deep in these departments, you should ask yourself, "Why?"

Especially if you rent predictive dialing equipment, a lot of the outbound calling can be done by the computer.

There is usually duplication of effort in the production area, particularly among supervisors. In marketing, the computer can assist with locating noncustomers, as we see in Stage Three.

I am not a machete wielder in the employee area. As a starter and a builder of companies, I am much more comfortable in creating jobs than in laying off people. It is expensive to terminate employees and frequently more advantageous and capital-creative to spin off good people into independent contractor organizations that can sell their services back to you.

SCORECARD

A 15% reduction in salaries for the $5 million (revenues) company, using the fairly broad average of $110,000 in revenues per employee—higher in high-tech and service industries—means a reduction of six people and a savings of approximately $180,000 per annum. A 15% reduction in salaries for the $20 million (revenues) company, using the same ratio, means a cut of 27 jobs or a savings of about $750,000 per annum. The savings will be much deeper if you use spin-offs or employee leasing. You have to choose the strategy that works for you.

Stage One Summary

The goal of Stage One is to help you triple your cash flow in 90 days. Did it happen? If you own or manage a $5 million (sales) company, I assume that your pretax profit is at best 5%, or $250,000; for the $20 million (sales) company, $1 million. In one quarter the cash flow for the small company is $62,500; tripled, it becomes $187,500. For the midsize company, one quarter's cash flow is $250,000; three times that amount is $750,000.

The cash windfall from Stage One ideas to the two sample companies and the three-month cash savings are:

Three months	Small company	Midsize company
(a) Cash saved	$277,651	$1,421,420
(b) Existing cash flow	62,500	250,000
ratio of (a)/(b)	4.4×	5.7×

It is unlikely that you will implement all of the cash-saving strategies in Stage One or that, if you do, you will achieve the exact savings cited in the first ten chapters. However, if you implement many of the ideas, you should achieve more than a threefold increase in cash flow.

Box Score Summary

	Revenues $5 million	Revenues $20 million
Rent		
Windfall	$ 61,151	$ 550,358
Annual savings	11,250	101,250
Communications	248,000	992,000
Health insurance	13,500	54,000
Legal services	10,000	25,000
Advertising	315,000	1,260,000
Loan costs	80,000	225,000
Accounting services	2,000	5,000
Travel costs	18,000	72,000
Supplier savings	(a)	(a)
Employee cuts	180,000	750,000
Total annual cost savings in cash	$866,000	$3,484,250

(a) Long-term savings only.

Stage Two
Spinning Off Peripheral Assets

11

Deciding What Is Core and What Is Peripheral

There is one and only one purpose for operating a business: to make your products or services a substitute for all other competitive products and services and to make all other competitive products and services no substitute for yours. Everyone who is in business tries to maximize his or her net returns. In trying to be efficient, entrepreneurs ask if what they are doing with their capital and their time is as sensible as something else they might be doing with them. They apply the principle of opportunity cost—the loss that is incurred by doing one thing instead of another that would have yielded some satisfaction. If you give up something in order to invest in an opportunity and realize a positive net return on an ongoing basis, that opportunity is *core*. In contrast, if you give up something to invest in another opportunity that does not produce positive net returns on an ongoing basis, that opportunity is *peripheral*.

I have developed a method of putting hard numbers on economic terms such as opportunity cost and positive net return. It comes from the venture capital business where new companies are launched with the goal of creating core businesses. It is not a foolproof test; nothing in business is foolproof. But it is an effective tool.

Silver's First Law of the Core

I have developed a fairly simple equation that defines a core business— one with a high and continuous net return on cost—and that distinguishes core businesses from peripheral ones. The equation—the First Law of the Core—is as follows:

$$V = P \times S \times M$$

where:

V   =   Valuation
P   =   The size of the problem that the company's products
        are solving
S   =   The elegance of the solution developed and marketed
        by the company
M   =   The quality of the management team

The creation and addition to wealth by commercial means is the result of three interrelated components:

1. The size of the problem (or "opportunity") that the business team has formulated
2. The elegance of the team's solution to that problem—that is, the uniqueness and appropriateness of the product or the nonduplicability of the marketing system
3. The competence of the management team

The greater the values one can achieve for P, S, and M, the greater will be the valuation of the company and the wealth of its stockholders. The three factors are interrelated. If all of them are large, the valuation will be very large. But if just one of them has a zero value, the venture (core or peripheral) will be worthless and the capital invested in it will be lost. Let's relate this simple but fundamental equation to three imaginary entrepreneurs who lived at the dawn of civilization:

> Far back among the mists of time, a family prepared for some important visitors from another tribe. In doing so, it created productivity, employment, and innovation.
> The family hunted and killed many birds, harvested vegetables, and picked fruit and coconuts to feed its guests. A friend was persuaded to cut down a tree and build a table and benches for the guests' comfort. Others were asked to clear an area in which the feast could be held. Still others were asked to cook, serve, and clear away the meal. All told, a dozen people worked on the feast, and the family promised each of them a reward when the feast was over.
> The feast was lavish and beautifully prepared. It tasted better than any meal the visitors had ever eaten. They promised to reciprocate, and a week later they sent the host family a fine goat as a thank-you present. The family gave goat's milk to all of the people who had helped prepare the feast. The workers were so pleased with the way the law of reciprocity worked that they eagerly volunteered to help prepare another feast, and another, and another.

As the feast business flourished and was transformed into a large-scale restaurant operation, however, some of the workers grew bored with performing the same tasks day after day. One of them, the table maker, left the first entrepreneur's team and built himself a floating table, which he called a boat. He planned to purchase food from the feast giver, load the food into his boat, transport it to nearby islands, and sell it to the tribes who lived there. The family of restaurant owners saw this enterprise as a second source of revenue, so it invested in the food exporting business.

Life is random, however, and rewards are uncertain. When the exporter arrived on the nearby island with his cargo of food, the tribe welcomed him with cries of joy and offered him a thousand coconuts as his reward. But it was not the food that they wanted, for they had plenty of that; it was his boat.

They explained to him that their island was heavily populated, a situation that had created a tremendous waste-removal problem. If the visitor would make boats for them, however, they would be able to cart their waste away easily.

Like many an entrepreneur in the centuries to follow, this food exporter found that he had to make a major change in his plans. There was no food shortage problem for him to solve, so he had to give up the export business. There was, however, a serious need for boats. Because all good entrepreneurs are flexible, the food exporter quickly transformed himself into a boat manufacturer. Also, this entrepreneur had learned management skills by working for the restaurateur, which give the M (management team) factor of his boat-making enterprise a high value. He had, in other words, all three components of the formula: a large problem, a good solution, and a competent* management team—himself and the workers he trained.

One of the boat maker's cleverest workers achieved a high-technology breakthrough: He invented the wheel. Initially, however, he had a very large S (solution) for which he had to find a P (problem)—or, preferably, several Ps. Eventually, he, too, decided to use his invention to solve the widespread problem of waste removal. To that end, he and his family began to produce wheelbarrows, which could be used to cart the waste to the shore where the second entrepreneur's boats waited. After firmly establishing his wheelbarrow business, he took advantage of many other commercial opportunities by setting up a waste-

*The words *competitive* and *competent* stem from the French root *competere*, which means "to be able to fly."

hauling enterprise, a wheel-manufacturing business, and dozens of other operations that relied on the wheel.

As the years passed, many other peripheral businesses were spun off from the original three. The circle of problem solving kept widening to include more and more solutions and customers (or receivers) of those solutions. Service organizations were established, and the manufacture of components became an important industry. The tribal people came to understand that their profits would exceed their costs by a significant margin as long as three circumstances prevailed:

1. The solutions had to solve large problems for the receivers.
2. The solutions had to be unique or presented in a unique, nonduplicable manner.
3. The law of reciprocity had to be obeyed to the letter.

Many inventor-entrepreneurs (like the one who invented the wheel) develop elegant solutions first and then find suitable problems for them. Note that the formulation of a problem is crucial, however, for no matter how elegant and unique the solution may be, it is of little or no value if there is not a serious problem. Contrary to Benjamin Franklin's claim, people will not beat a path to your door if you develop a better mousetrap, for that is a solution that lacks a serious problem.

Multiple revenue sources exist for each of the three companies in the story. Competent management teams are capable of multiplying their V (wealth) by introducing new Ss and offering them to the established receivers by unique methods. For example, the family of restaurateurs could open additional restaurants on nearby islands, sell franchises to tribes on faraway islands, package their delicacies for sale at boat docks, launch a gourmet magazine, and publish their recipes. The boat manufacturer could start a rent-a-boat business or operate boats under contract for tribes that prefer to have their transport needs managed by someone more experienced than themselves. The wheelbarrow manufacturer could establish a wheelbarrow rental agency, operate a garbage removal business under contract with tribes who prefer that service, and exploit his wheel as a component part of other products.

There is a rule of thumb that for every job created by a new commercial enterprise, one additional job is created in the community to service the employee and his or her family. These jobs are filled by new service businesses employing teachers, beauticians, clerks, service station attendants, and the like.

Note the myriad services for which these first three companies created a need. The restaurant created a need for laundry and linen supply services, printers to supply menus, graphic artists to design signs and menus, garbage removal services, suppliers of fresh flowers for restaurant tables, furniture manufacturers, musicians to provide ambiance, manufacturers of uniforms for the waiters and waitresses, and advertising and public relations services to inform customers about their service. With further expansion, the first entrepreneurs will require day-care services for their employees' children, lawyers to draft franchising agreements, and a marketing team to sell their delicacies at boat docks and to sell franchises to faraway tribes.

The services created by the second company, the boat maker, include leasing consultants, travel agents to schedule trips for the boat maker's sales personnel, bankers to open letters of credit, and facilities management consultants to assist the entrepreneur in pricing and operating his transportation management services to other islands.

The third company, the inventor, needs assistance in industrial design because his wheels, which are made of coconuts, have a tendency to crack when a heavy load is carted in the wheelbarrow. He also needs engineers, financial consultants, and management consultants. Inventor-entrepreneurs seem to require the greatest number of service professionals to fill the gaps in their knowledge.

Another development often occurs as new companies sprout up: the parent company and/or local citizens receive an opportunity to invest in them. In many instances, however, the sponsoring investors lose their investment because they mistakenly assign positive values to P, S, and M, when zero is in fact the correct value.

Putting the Formula to Work

The formula $V = P \times S \times M$ is the fundamental law of the core process. It explains why some new enterprises succeed and others fail. Assume, for example, that the maximum value for P, S, and M is 3 and that their minimum value is 0. Then the greatest commercial opportunity would have an initial score of 27 ($V = 3 \times 3 \times 3$). On the other hand, the worst opportunity would have an initial score of 0 (but that zero could be arrived at in many ways: $1 \times 1 \times 0 = 0$; $0 \times 2 \times 3 = 0$; $3 \times 0 \times 3 = 0$; and so forth). Between these two extreme scores are the majority of commercial opportunities: those toward the high end tend to become core businesses and those toward the low end, peripheral businesses. The $3 \times 3 \times 3$ situations are extremely rare, although they have occurred on perhaps 75 occasions, by my estimation, in the last twenty-five years. The V factors of these 75 companies average approximately $5 billion, and the companies were each launched with less than $150,000 in up-front capital. Ten of them are described in Exhibit 11-1.

Exhibit 11-1. New companies with high overall V.

Name of Company	Founded	Description of Business	Start-up Capital	1993 V ($ millions)
1. Wal-Mart Stores	1962	Discount stores	Personal savings	$35,000
2. Microsoft	1976	Computer software	Personal savings	27,000
3. McDonald's	1961	Fast food	Personal savings	14,200
4. Sony	1946	Pocket electronics	Personal savings	13,500
5. Intel	1968	Semiconductors	$2 million	12,000
6. Holiday Inns of America	1952	Motel chain	Personal savings	8,700
7. Turner Broadcasting	1978	Cable broadcasting	$500,000	8,000
8. McCaw Cellular	1981	Cellular telephones	$1 million	5,700
9. Genentech	1977	Genetic engineering	$1 million	5,400
10. Electronic Data Systems	1962	Facilities management	$20,000	2,500

A close examination of the P, S, and M of those ten companies will show you why they have achieved such high valuations: The value of all three factors in the formula was extremely high for each company.

To further demonstrate the utility of the first law of entrepreneurship, let's look at some of the greatest business failures of recent memory and see which of the factors—P, S, or M—was missing (see Exhibit 11-2).

Bear in mind that some fairly experienced venture capital investors perceived these companies as having positive values in their P, S, and M accounts, when in fact at least one of the factors was worth zero in each company listed in Exhibit 11-2.

In the case of DeLorean Motor Company, it is generally believed that *all* of the factors had either zero or almost zero values.

Let's examine those factors one at a time. First of all, the problem DeLorean formulated—a need for expensive sports cars—was nonexistent. Porsche, Jaguar, Nissan, and other manufacturers were already battling fiercely for the attention of the $25,000-and-up car buyer, and there was simply no need for another manufacturer to enter the field. In this instance, then, P equaled zero.

As for the second factor, DeLorean provided a solution that was not unique, and he proceeded to market that solution in a way that was easily duplicable. Thus, S also equaled zero.

The M factor—the management team—did appear to have positive value during the start-up phase of the company. John Z. DeLorean, by all measures, was a corporate achiever with a distinguished track record at General Motors. With his departure from GM and the publication of his book, *On a Clear Day You Can See General Motors*, it appeared that DeLorean was making the traditional passage from dissatisfied, bored

Exhibit 11-2. Large commercial failures of the 1980s and 1990s.

Name of Company	Date Founded	Type of Business	Wasted ($000)	Primary Investors
1. DeLorean Motor Company	1978	Expensive cars	$134,000	R&D LP
2. U. S. Football League	1982	Sports league	120,000	Private
3. Ibis Corporation	1983	Minicomputers	85,000	Vent. Cap.
4. Air Florida	1979	Regional airline	75,000	Vent. Cap.
5. Z-Tel	1983	Telephone equipment	56,000	Vent. Cap.
6. Florida Data Corporation	1982	Minicomputers	35,000	Vent. Cap.
7. Osborne Computer Corporation	1982	Portable computers	25,000	Vent. Cap.
8. Mindset Corporation	1983	Personal computers	18,500	Vent. Cap.
9. Gavilan Computer	1983	Laptop computers	15,000	Vent. Cap.
10. Otrona Corporation	1983	Portable computers	15,000	Vent. Cap.

manager to driven, energetic, self-fulfilled entrepreneur. The rapid demise of his automobile company and the steps that he took to save it have since raised serious questions about DeLorean's competence, but in the early days, the M factor must have looked very attractive. Nonetheless, even if his management team deserved a 3, when this value was multiplied by the two zeros in the P and S accounts, the result would have been a clear and resounding valuation of zero.

The DeLorean example vividly illustrates the importance of formulating a very large P, developing a unique S (either protected by patents or conveyed to the market in an innovative manner), and assembling a management team that includes one or more corporate achievers.

Each of these three factors—problem, solution, and management team—is vital to the success of the enterprise. In fact, the demise of many businesses, both small and large, is a direct result of the neglect of one or more of the factors.

If the P factor is relatively small, the commercial opportunity should be discarded. It is extremely expensive (read advertising dollars) to persuade people to buy something that they do not need. Attempting behavior modification via advertising is one of the fastest ways to waste large amounts of capital. But if the P factor is large and the development of the S factor—the patented or proprietary product or the unique and nonduplicable delivery channel—will require time and capital, then you have an outstanding candidate for a highly profitable peripheral division spin-off.

12

Spinning Off Peripheral Divisions to Their Employees

If you have at least 45 employees, some of them are very likely engaged in peripheral activities not related directly to the daily routine of producing and delivering your product. If these people have an enterpreneurial spirit, you should spin them off. But there is a right way and a wrong way to do it. One strategy for generating capital to support the core business is to spin off entrepreneurial departments and factories via management buyouts and facilities management contracts, thereby eliminating the overhead that accompanies these operations. This strategy is most successful when outside capital is needed to develop the peripheral business to its fullest potential. When the skills of the workers join with the combustible enthusiasm of an entrepreneurial shop where the workers own a piece of the action, the former sole parent (which retains part ownership of the spin-off) can benefit from:

- The capital gain from selling a substantial part of the division
- The familiarity of having a subcontract manufacturer with known managers and employees
- A second capital gain when the spun-off division achieves a public offering or is acquired.

Express Scripts, which offers pharmacy benefit management services, including integrated mail order and local retail pharmacy network services, was partially spun off from New York Life Insurance Company in June 1992, when approximately 27.5% of its shares were sold to the public for $26 million, thereby valuing New York Life's investment at more than $75 million (a significant increase from the $4.2 million that New York Life was carrying on its books). Sales in 1991 had been $47 million, on which the company earned $2.9 million.

Thermo Electron, a manufacturer of environmental and analytic instruments, industrial process equipment, and drug detection devices, has $800 million in revenues. It has adopted a strategy of selling a minority interest in subsidiary companies, creating, as of this writing, Thermedics, Thermo Instrument Systems, Thermo Process Systems, Thermo Electron Technologies, and Tecogen, all publicly held subsidiaries of Thermo Electron. The prospectus for the parent's newest spin-off, Thermo Cardiosystems, states that one of Thermo Electron's reasons for the spin-off strategy is its belief that it has "enhanced the entrepreneurial environment for employees of the company." The parent leases facilities and shares resources with its subsidiaries, as well as with centralized administrative, banking, and credit services under a five-year renewable blanket charter.

The most elegant peripheral division spin-off, and the one mastered by Thermo Electron, is to sell your divisions to their management teams *while retaining a piece of the action.* The management buyout (MBO) has become a popular cash-raising strategy in the age of corporate downsizing. There are several hundred sources of equity and debt financing eager to back a management team that crosses over to an entrepreneurial team.

The Management Buyout

Management buyouts are generally preferred by lenders to leveraged buyouts because managers have more experience running their divisions than do the hired guns brought into the division by outside raiders. This means there is an ample supply of capital available to managers who wish to buy a division from you. A second reason often cited by lenders for liking MBOs is that division managers frequently enjoy a privileged position with the parent company's management, which translates into the parent's willingness to extend itself to help the division managers buy the company. Although there is some truth to this, the reality is more like this: Division managers have less experience than do outside corporate raiders in financing management buyouts, and they need the seller to carry notes as part of the selling price.

The process for assessing the feasibility of an MBO is presented in Exhibit 12-1.

Exhibit 12-1. Assessing the feasibility of an MBO.

1. Obtain liquidation or quick-sale value appraisals for all of the division's assets, both on the balance sheet and off.
2. Apply conventional loan ratios against these values:
   (a) 100% of cash, marketable securities, and cash surrender value of life insurance
   (b) 80 to 90% of accounts receivable
   (c) 50 to 60% of raw material and finished goods inventory
   (d) 75 to 80% of plant, equipment, and land
   (e) 80% of customer list
   The sum of (a) through (e) equals total leverage; add an overadvance equal to 25% of total leverage if the company's earnings before interest and taxes (EBIT) are strong, that is, 25% of revenues or more.
3. Multiply the total loan by the prime rate plus 4%, the estimated interest rate on asset-based loans.
4. Amortize the fixed-asset loans and customer list loan equally over seven years, beginning with the thirteenth month following the MBO. Assume the current asset loan revolves.
5. Add to net profit before taxes the following operating statement amounts:
   (a) Interest
   (b) Depreciation
   (c) Amortization
   (d) Corporate surcharges
   (e) Needless overhead (the key to the deal!)
   The sum of (a) through (e) equals adjusted EBIT (total these amounts and you have cash flow, or adjusted EBIT, as the takeover entrepreneurs call it).
6. If adjusted EBIT exceeds total annual debt service by more than 1.3 times, the management team will be able to service the takeover debt.
7. Caveat: If there is existing debt on the division's balance sheet, deduct the amount of existing debt from total leverage because it must be repaid.

An MBO in the Sports Optics Field

Rifle scopes and swimming goggles have very little in common except for being round, made of clear plastic or glass, and used to enhance vision in shooting and swimming. Lachman Optical Manufacturing (not the real name), founded at the turn of the century, began as an optical equipment manufacturing company and over three generations grew to sales of $15 million, of which $10 million was from rifle scopes and $5 million was from swimming goggles. Both lines are profitable, but the goggle business was not growing, and its profit margins were shrinking. The marketing channels for the two products were entirely different: hunting and outdoor sports equipment stores for the rifle scopes and coaches, direct-mail catalogs, resorts, and sports apparel stores for the swimming goggles. Kevin Lachman, the CEO, liked the diversity that the counterseasonal businesses offered. But when it took more and more advertising dollars to deliver $4.9 million in revenues from the goggle line in 1992, roughly the same as the prior year, he thought about selling it.

The merger and acquisition consultant at my firm with whom Kevin met asked if the division's management team might want to buy the swimming goggles division. Kevin and the consultant met with the management team, and they reviewed the feasibility, price, and possible structure of an MBO. Kevin wanted $3.5 million in cash for the division, and we advised him to hold onto 20% so that he would gain if the goggle division was resold at a higher price or achieved in initial public offering.

The division's $1.1 million in accounts receivable and $850,000 in accounts receivable inventory attracted $1.5 million in loans, and the management team raised $1 million in venture capital. They had $350,000 in cash from personal savings, bringing them to $2.85 million, or 80% of the $3.5 million asking price. Thus, the deal went through, with the team acquiring 80% of the business. The division's cash flow the next year was $350,000 before interest on the new debt of $150,000 per annum. One year after the spin-off, the goggles company sold its manufacturing equipment for $500,000 and contracted the manufacturing work to a Mexican factory, lowering production costs. It bought a flipper line and began manufacturing polystyrene training equipment to broaden its line. It began publishing its own catalog aimed at coaches and teams and cut all advertising. Earnings grew to $1 million pretax. By mid-1993, underwriters were seen hovering around, itching to take the company public.

13

Facilities Management Spin-Offs

I once visited a guardrail manufacturer with sales of $11.3 million that was going nowhere. Its CEO was pulling his hair out looking for new markets. He was beginning to make some strides in marketing recreational park handrails and handrails for housing for the elderly and the disabled, but these diversifications took time and capital. The company was heavily borrowed and because of a weak bottom line could not attract venture capital.

The CEO had cut expenses to the bone, and he was desperately looking for ways to hold on until the new marketing channels kicked in with what he believed would be—and convinced me would be—big orders. He asked me for advice. I noticed that his data processing department had been pioneering in CAD software for several years to come up with efficient and inexpensive handrails for the elderly and the disabled.

Their renderings of railing systems in CAD had numerous applications in the design, industrial engineering, and architectural fields. I asked the CEO if the people in the data-processing department were entrepreneurial. He said, "Well, they work mostly noon to midnight, come in on weekends, never go out for lunch, order in junk food, keep coming up with applications for other markets, and pretty much stick to themselves."

I responded, "Sounds like a software start-up to me. Do they have a leader?"

"Yes, Janie Smythe. Want to meet her?"

We met with Janie, and she thought that the team might go for a facilities management spin-off. As a group the team billed the company about $3 million per annum for everything—salaries, computer rental, software purchases, utilities, and space.

The company agreed to pay the spun-off unit $2.75 million per annum in quarterly installments for its services for three years (the savings came from Social Security, medical insurance, and other benefits). The spun-off company—Janie named it Fac-Man Computing—would continue to perform services for the company but had the right to seek business from other clients. The parent company maintained a 20% interest in Fac-Man in consideration for having its finance department do the books and tax returns and pay the checks for Fac-Man for two years.

Fac-Man moved into its own space in six months when it had won a couple of outside contracts, and the parent company rented Fac-Man's former space to a small environmental engineering services company to which it charged rent and with which it co-ventured on bids to the National Park Service.

The facilities management spin-off has been used in markets other than data processing. Money management companies, for example, have used it frequently and with considerable success. For example, the investment department of Chemical Bank, New York, was responsible for $9.5 billion in assets under management for trust customers at the time of its spin-off. The department is managed by a team that is employed by and has an equity interest in Favia, Hill & Co., a management company. James A. Favia and his partner, John Hill, who once headed Chemical Bank's investment department, negotiated with the bank's top management and agreed to run the $9.5 billion investment department as proper fiduciaries—not as employees of the bank but as stockholders of a new money management company, Favia, Hill. Now Favia and Hill can sell their stock-picking skills to new clients, grow their company to any size they like, and take it public or sell it back to Chemical Bank or to the highest bidder.

How might this work out? Assume that a money management firm charges its customers .5% of the total assets under management. Also assume that a company with $3 billion under management has gross income of $15 million. If 100 people at an average salary of $75,000 per annum are employed to manage the $3 billion and if another $500,000 per annum is spent on investigation costs, then the net profit to the owners of the company is $7 million. If the assets under management double to $6 billion and if only 25 employees are added to the payroll, net profits to the owners will grow to $20 million. An owner of 10% of the stock of the money management company would receive a dividend of $2 million for doing the same job he or she once earned bank wages for doing.

Favia and Hill are two of the many money management department heads of commercial banks who have used the facilities management spin-off to establish separate companies. The venture capital industry is composed of some 625 firms, about 5% of which were launched using this strategy. The fashion industry is dotted with designers who design apparel lines under contract to manufacturers as well as for their own label.

Federal and state governments are beginning to express interest in facilities management. The agencies that they seem most willing to spin off to entrepreneurs are the less attractive ones, such as waste removal and prison management.

The Power of Spin-Offs

When a spin-off is being considered, the parent has all the leverage. Most senior managers do not understand how to use this leverage, however. They either react impulsively and fire the department managers for disloyalty or they name the price, the terms, and the closing date by which the spin-off must be effected. This, in turn, forces the manager-entrepreneurs to scramble to raise the money, an area in which they have little experience.

If senior managers knew how to implement leverage, they could hold on to equity in the spun-off company, which could well become more valuable than its parent. This can happen when the spin-off's ability to solve (S) the problem (P), elegantly exceeds that of its parent. Given equal management abilities (M), the spun-off company's value generally eventually exceeds that of the parent.

The second value driver is that former managers frequently make outstanding entrepreneurs because they combine years of experience and the emotional thrill of owning their own company. The combination is intoxicating and frequently brings out the best talents of managers of divisional spin-offs.

Retaining the Leveraging Opportunity

When Itek Corporation was purchased by Raytheon Corporation for $350 million in 1988, I was reminded once again of a traditionally managed corporation that lost a leveraging opportunity. In the late 1960s a small cluster of engineers at Eastman Kodak Corporation presented some innovative product ideas in the field of optics to senior management. They were turned down and soon left to start Itek (the punch line is that Itek stands for "I'll take Eastman Kodak"). The capital gain earned by the founders of Itek could have been

Eastman Kodak's if Kodak's senior management had understood the leverage in spin-offs.

When a new employee is hired and given his or her employee handbook, I recommend that, along with the rules and regulations on ethics, the health care insurance plan, and vacation leave, the following information be given:

> If, in the course of your employment at ABC Industries, you develop an innovative idea or a skill that you believe ABC can market to others, we encourage you to bring it to the attention of your senior managers. We welcome entrepreneurial ideas, and we would prefer to help you develop and test the ideas within the company, rather than have you leave us because you feel the company is not receptive to innovation.

By encouraging entrepreneurship and then assisting employees with their spin-offs, companies can meet their own needs for growth and innovation while earning a capital gain.

14

Sale-Leaseback of Fixed Assets

One of the most common ways to squeeze cash out of fixed assets is to sell them to a leasing company and then lease them back. This tactic is called the sale-leaseback, and it is routinely done by traditional corporations whenever their financial situation is looking increasingly grim.

Sale-Leaseback of Office Space

To find sale-leaseback investors for your office building or warehouse, begin with investors who seek high-quality buildings, and, if necessary, run down the list to lower-quality investors. Somewhere along the way, you should find the right match.

Insurance companies are the most likely real estate investors. Other candidates are corporate pension funds, college endowment funds, and association or small pension funds. At the lower end of the quality scale are wealthy individuals herded into syndicates by investment bankers. Although there is an overhead cost in selling your asset to them—individuals die, get divorced, or want special reports sent hither and thither—the sale does free up cash.

A Sample Sale-Leaseback Arrangement: Delivery Vans

Let's assume you own a fleet of 20 delivery vans with which you service customers. Each van costs you $15,000. You can sell the vans for $7,500 each, or $150,000. The cost of owning and operating the 20 vans is shown in Exhibit 14-1.

If your company delivers goods to customers, you want to do it

Exhibit 14-1. Cost of owning and operating 20 vans.

	1 Van	20 Vans
Approximate monthly payment for a 60-month loan at 10.75% with 15% down payment	$ 276	$ 5,520
Liability insurance	125	2,500
Maintenance	100	2,000
Gas (1,500 miles per month, 15 miles/gallon @ 85 cents/gallon	85	1,700
Driver (20 hours/week @ $8/hour)	640	12,800
Workers' compensation	102	2,040
Drivers' health insurance	120	2,400
Total	$1,448	$28,960

the most cost-effective way. The choices are owning, leasing and providing the drivers, leasing both the vans and the drivers, using common carriers, and giving the fleet management department a facilities management contract. In Chapter 10 we examined employee leasing, which has numerous cost-saving features. The facilities management option offers your company the opportunity to maintain a risk-free, cost-free equity interest in the fleet-management company. Both of these two options free up space and lower costs by about the same amount.

Subcontracting the delivery function to a common carrier represents an even heftier savings. The estimated common carrier costs are presented in Exhibit 14-2.

In general, if you ship less than a truckload, it is more cost-effective to use common carriers. For example, if your company ships loads of from 250 to 500 pounds per van to customers 20 times per week within a 50-mile radius of your warehouse and if the products are Class 70 (general freight, that is, cosmetics, pens, office supplies) with a retail value of $5,000 per load, using a common carrier is less expensive than owning or leasing the vans or trucks (see Exhibit 14-3). However, if you can consolidate your shipments and build delivery costs into the price of the products, then owning or leasing your vans or trucks and offering backhaul services provides greater flexibility.

Leasing the vans and employing the drivers and leasing both the vans and the drivers are the remaining two options. We already know that employee leasing and van leasing will be the least expensive of

Exhibit 14-2. Cost of using a common carrier.

	1 Van	20 Vans
50 miles @ 95 cents, 20 loads/month*	$950	$19,000
Insurance (40 cents per $100 of value; cost for a		
$5,000 load)	20	400
Total	$970	$19,400

*Charges for a delivery service range from per-mile charges to flat fees determined by weight and value of shipment. The average cost is 95 cents/mile.

these two options; thus, we look at the cost of that option only (see Exhibit 14-3).

This option frees up $13,320 in cash in the first month. However, beginning in the second month it costs $31,680 per month, which is 50% higher than the common carrier option. The sale produces $45,000 in immediate cash but does not provide a cash flow annuity as does the common carrier option. The facilities management option may produce a long-term capital gain, but that is uncertain.

None of these options factors in the revenue features of *backhauling* for others, a gatekeeper management approach to the cost of trucks and vans. PepsiCo's Frito Lay trucks sport brightly colored ads on their rear ends advertising Frito Lay's backhauling services and providing an 800 telephone number for prospects to call for information.

Exhibit 14-3. Cost of using sale-leaseback of vans and leasing the drivers.

	1 Van	20 Vans
Return of 15% down payment on vans and		
investment of proceeds at 10% per year	$(2,250)	$(45,000)
60-month lease at 21.5%	552	11,040
Driver (20 hours/week @ $8/hour)	807	16,140
Liability insurance	125	2,500
Maintenance	100	2,000
Workers' compensation	(a)	(a)
Drivers' health insurance	(a)	(a)
Total	$ (660)	$(13,320)

(a) Imbedded in driver leasing costs.

15

Renting Out
Freed-Up Space

By this time, you have freed up a considerable amount of office, plant, and warehouse space that you can rent to other companies.

Seek Tenants in Related Businesses

After moving desks, computers, telephones, and fax machines to more efficient locations, let's assume that you have 5,000 square feet on two floors to rent to other companies. For security reasons, you want tenants that do not have walk-in customers. They may need conference room facilities and lots of telephone lines. Thanks to call-accounting systems, they can use your telephone system and the bills can be separate. Other mechanics of the tenancy can be negotiated in a cooperative spirit.

There are ideal tenants whose presence can add demonstrable value to your company. For example, if your company manufactures nationally branded consumer products, a tenant in one of the following areas could pay for its lease ten times over with advice and assistance:

- Bartering company
- Broker of billboard space
- Broker of radio spots
- Marketer of consumer plugs in motion pictures
- Shared-mail marketer
- Consumer research company
- Artificial intelligence software company
- Telemarketing company
- Target marketing company
- Catalog marketing company

The personnel in these companies could perform intelligence-gathering services that could flatten the learning curve for your senior management in these innovative fields.

Similarly, if your company develops high-technology products, you might want to sublease space to a legal firm specializing in patent law; if your company has a lot of people on the road at all times, consider renting space to a travel club operator. But you get the point. Use the *leverage* in your potential client relationship to select companies as sublet tenants. Then use their ideas and their services in exchange for *soft dollars,* which means that you pay in services rather than in cash.

A typical soft-dollar deal might state that you will get free market research in exchange for free parking, janitorial services, electricity, heat, insurance, and use of the conference room. Wall Street brokerage firms trade research on stocks with institutional investors to get their orders. You might provide mail presorting services, bundling the tenant's mail with yours, for a tenant whose monthly mail volume is too small to presort. You can serve as a PPO for your subtenants to lower their health insurance costs, and an aggrogator to lower their express mail, travel, and delivery costs. In exchange for these services, you could ask for the following services:

- Lead generation
- List rental
- Public relations
- Legal services
- Export assistance

The number of potential relationships boggles the imagination. Carl Marks & Company, New York, a market maker in foreign securities, has operated a leveraged buyout and mezzanine financing firm for 25 years. It spawned two well-known raiders, John Jordan, who bought more than 40 companies in five years, and Joseph Steinberg, who took over James Talcott, the commercial finance company now known as Leucadia, and is frequently in the bidding action when a traditionally managed corporation is in play. Carl Marks rented two offices in the early 1970s to "supplier" tenants. One was Herbert B. Max, generally regarded as one of the premier lawyers in the field of acquisitions and divestitures. Max was only a few feet away when a deal needed discussion. He had outside clients, but Carl Marks received special attention.

I was the other tenant. My apparent value was that I generated a number of books, articles, and speeches that stimulated quite a large deal flow, through which Carl Marks had the right to sift. The relationship worked well for all parties, and we each took something from the others while giving services in return.

With five subtenants, each with 10 to 20 employees, it is conceivable that you may have sufficient clout to negotiate with outside providers for lower costs for a variety of operating expenses items, as well as cutting your share of the cost of physical facilities and electronic equipment within your office. The negotiable operational areas might include costs for couriers and health insurance, shared mail marketing, and vehicle leasing. The savings could result in additional cash flow to your company on top of rent and the information value of having innovative tenants a few steps away with their eyes and ears keenly tuned to opportunities that could benefit your business.

The production employees of Kone Instruments, a clinical lab instrument manufacturer in Estpool, Finland, formed a corporation in 1992 in which they are the sole stockholders, and they entered into a contract to manufacture clinical lab instruments for Kone. The result for Kone is a savings in cost of goods sold.

Keep the Relationship Clear and Specific

The key to successful subtenant relationships based on the exchange of services is to write a standard lease, albeit at a reduced rent, and to specify in the rider the responsibilities of each party—for example, "The landlord will provide telephone equipment, photocopying equipment, personal computers, fax machines and supplies, and conference facilities at no cost to the tenant."

The tenant's responsibilities might be stated as follows: "Tenant shall search, review, and file all patents for the landlord in a timely manner at one-half tenant's customary billing rate." Additional riders can be added as the need arises.

Summarizing the Spin-Off Strategy

Before actually undertaking a spin-off, it is advisable to pull together a small group of managers and at least one outside consultant who has overseen some spin-offs and who has nothing to lose by speaking his or her mind. The group's skills must include knowing how to spin off assets that are not essential to the company's core. Each spin-off is different in its mechanics; the group must understand the different kinds of spin-offs and the different ways the parent company can profit from the spin-off while giving up risk and costs.

Deciding to sell a manufacturing subsidiary that never was part of the company's core is a simple judgment call and should be done quickly. The group also will have to make tougher calls, however, such as spinning off divisions that service the company (data processing, human resources, advertising), not because they do not fit but because spinning them off raises cash. These three spin-offs are seldom done by traditional managers; if done at all, they are not done well.

The optimum facilities management spin-off is of a service department that manages an internal generic activity extremely well, a department that other corporations that have a need for the service would hire to provide services to them if it were freestanding. Most facilities management spin-offs have involved the data-processing departments of large and medium-size corporations.

In the facilities management spin-off, the budget of the department leaves the parent, thus freeing up cash, and the spun-off division agrees with the parent to provide its usual services on a contract basis. The spun-off division incorporates, and the former employees of the parent become employees of the new entity, which is free to provide services to other companies and has the endorsement of the parent as it tries to obtain outside contracts. Working capital for the spun-off division is provided by service contracts from the parent company and from others. Smart corporations hold onto some equity in the spun-off companies because these companies occasionally become valuable.

The consulting group should review the various divisions carefully to determine which have the greatest spin-off possibilities. Successful facilities management spin-offs must provide a service that other companies can use, must be made up of an enthusiastic, high-energy entrepreneurial group of employees, and must be willing to take the risk when the umbilical cord is cut.

Stage Three
Putting the Zip Back in Marketing

16

Finding Your Product's Demonstrable Economic Proposition

What is the difference between one word processing package and another? Between one bank loan and another? Between one oscilloscope and another? Every product or service has at least one unique feature that distinguishes it from its competitors.

In selling real estate, the experts say that location is the most important factor. In venture capital, the experts say that management is the most important single factor and that, no matter what business a company is in, bad management will wreck it and good management will save it. (There are also those who say that certain businesses are "idiot-proof"; that is, the need for them is so great and the solution they offer so unique that no management team can kill them.)

Ask yourself what it is that makes your company's product line unique. What is it that makes it a substitute for competitive products and makes competitive products no substitute for yours? What is its *demonstrable economic proposition*, or DEP factor?

The DEP factor may be that your products or services, though equal in efficiency to competitive products, are faster in delivering results. Or your product may be less expensive than competitive products, although it is neither more efficient nor faster. The DEP factor may be that, while your products or services are not effective, your competitors' products are much worse. Your product may last longer or be easier to use, or you may deliver them more efficiently.

One way to find out why people buy your product or use your service is to *ask* them. There are many ways to ask customers why they are customers, but remember this: They are experts about one or two aspects of your product or service. When you put a dozen of their opinions together, you have a consensus about the demonstrable economic proposition of your product. Listen to your *users*. If you listen to your marketing managers, you may be misled by their fear of telling you the truth. This is known as the Pirandello problem, named for the playwright who wrote about the king who went outside without clothes but whose subjects would not tell him because they feared his wrath. In addition, sales managers are frequently interested in obtaining larger budgets and in persuading management to spend more money on advertising to help them make more sales, which puts more money in their pockets.

Fortunately, because of the microchip, it is possible to gather feedback from customers and noncustomers alike at the point of purchase, that is, when they are thinking about your product's utility or lack of it.

Learning From Bounceback

One of my favorite images is of a young child quietly playing alone with a rubber ball on a summer morning, bouncing it off something that brings it back to him or her. A ball bounced off the side of a building goes over the child's head if it is bounced too high and bounces straight down and hugs the wall if the child throws it into a crack or a crevice. The point is this: The bounceback conveys more information about the thrown ball than the throwing of the ball does. In fact, if you think about someone throwing curves, sliders, and knuckleballs at the wall so that the ball bounces back in unsuspected ways, it's clear that the bounceback conveys all of the information about the thrown ball.

When you put a product or a service into the market, you are like a child throwing a rubber ball against a wall and gleefully chasing its unknown bounce. With repeated throws of the ball, the information begins to form certain truths, and the child becomes adept at throwing and catching. So, too, with a new product. Throw it into the market and watch what happens; you can learn about the product by immediately asking customers and noncustomers why they bought it or did not buy it.

The Power of Headlines

I like to shop. I like to shop for food, pharmaceuticals, health and beauty aids, office supplies, housewares and appliances, house renovation tools, books, sporting goods, and airline tickets. I go shopping several times a week, and I am not put off by long checkout lines, poorly trained store clerks, or out-of-stock inventory. I like clutter in stores. I like to people-watch in stores. And one of my favorite things to do is to browse through the *National Enquirer* while waiting at the checkout counter.

Whoever writes the headlines for the *National Enquirer* (or the *Star* or the *World*) has a sense of what catches the imagination of the typical consumer. Everyone I know, when asked to recite three *National Enquirer* headlines, can do so inside of 60 seconds. Yet, if I ask the same people to recite the headlines of their three favorite product advertisements, they usually cannot do it. If they can, it takes them considerably longer than recalling *Enquirer* headlines.

I did not discover this fact. It has occurred to quite a few executives who want to become better headline writers. They gain more ideas for headlines from key words in *National Enquirer* headlines than their staff members are able to provide. Toss a few of these words around to see how they might fit into a statement that incorporates most of the reasons that consumers use your product or service:

alien	monster	home
mob	kill	skinned
alive	free	beast
birth	stroke	blood
bomb	kiss	fight

These are words we use in everyday conversation. They are simple, yet descriptive. But you rarely see them or the image that they describe in the headline of a statement that sets forth the DEP factor of a product or service.

Have you ever read a copy of the *National Enquirer* or one of the other tabloids? The fact is that the stories for the most part are about personal achievement, wellness, weight loss, and money-making schemes. It is a service magazine; its readers go behind the headline to read about becoming a better person.

The same is true with *Playboy*, whose "headline" is female nudity. *Playboy* was conceived as a magazine to advise young men on how to dress, act, speak to women, order in a restaurant, and avoid acting as if they had just come off the farm. At the time that Hugh Hefner launched *Playboy*, when young men were beginning to leave small towns in droves and seek their fortunes in the cities, *Playboy* served its purpose well, and it continues to do so.

The *National Enquirer* and *Playboy* are not the only products whose covers belie the message of the book but without which covers, the books would be less well read. IBM, most computer users will tell you, rarely produced the best computers, but the headlines of their advertisements oozed service, user friendliness, and the security of protection within the IBM family. (How times change! Despite the friendliness of its message, IBM found itself outpaced technologically by makers whose computers really offered what IBM promised—ease of use at reasonable cost.)

All of us know the great headlines; the ones that make a proposition that we cannot ignore. Headlines that have become magnets. Headlines that persuade. Headlines that assure. Headlines that entice us into entering the company's space.

"Membership has its privileges." "The ultimate driving machine." "Pardon me. Do you have any Grey Poupon?"

Headline Writing

In attempting to find an award-winning headline, return to the formula $V = P \times S \times M$; but ignore the M factor unless your company has a spokesperson with the down-home qualities of Frank Perdue (IT TAKES A TOUGH MAN TO MAKE A TENDER CHICKEN). You have three factors to work with: the size of the problem (P), the elegance of your solution (S), or the wealth (V) that your solution will generate for consumers of your (S).

Successful P-based headlines include THE HEARTBREAK OF PSORIASIS, the invention of the word "halitosis" that gave a name to bad breath and provided an enemy for Listerine to fight, and I CAN'T BELIEVE I ATE THE WHOLE THING, which sold lots of Alka-Seltzer in its day.

Winning S-based headlines—and most companies lean on the S more than the P to describe their validity—include THE ULTIMATE DRIVING MACHINE for BMW automobiles, YOU CAN TRUST YOUR CAR TO THE MAN WHO WEARS THE STAR for Texaco gasoline, and LOOK, MA, NO CAVITIES for Crest toothpaste. The propositions stated in these headlines are every bit as riveting as ELVIS SPOTTED COMING OUT OF A BURGER KING or an equivalent *National Enquirer* headline.

Try your hand at writing a new headline for your company's product or service. Begin in antique stores.

To find some of the best headlines, buy a dozen or more magazines from the 1950s at your local antique store. The 1950s seem to have a lot in common with the 1990s—both are times of healing and pulling loose ends together following a bombastic, chaotic decade. Many of the headlines of the 1950s may work in the 1990s.

The Lucky Strike headline SO ROUND, SO FIRM, SO FULLY PACKED, SO FREE AND EASY ON THE DRAW is a grandiose statement about a small item. YOU MEET THE NICEST PEOPLE ON A HONDA helped launch mopeds in the United States.

Are you confident that your product or service will work every time for the user? If so, offer a money-back guarantee. Are you extremely confident that your product or service will solve the user's problem every single time he or she uses it? If so, why not offer a double-your-money-back-if-not-completely-satisfied guarantee? That is headline enough.

Be sure your gross profit margin is sufficiently large to handle a 5 to 10% return rate from creeps who order your product for the sole purpose of returning it to double their money.

Summary

Rethink your headline. You may be making a statement about P when the potential customer base is focused on a demand for S. Or you may be stressing the mechanical construction of your product when potential customers are pulling their hair out about a P that they wish they could solve. How do you find out which way to go? Ask them. Have them fill out a bounceback card inserted into the product. To get a better bounceback, call up a few customers and ask them why they bought your product. Or have a field person ask them at the point of purchase. Remember: The bounceback brings you more information than the throw.

17

Multiplying Your Marketing Channels

Marketing channels sometimes take years and millions of dollars to create. Even if you have some cash on hand, hold onto it. I want to show you how to create *multiple cash-flow channels* without spending very much cash.

How many businesses do you know that sell their product or service through one marketing channel? Not many. Even physicians have taken up newsletter publishing to find new patients. Accountants sponsor tax and new-ventures seminars where they can troll for new clients. Book publishers have gone beyond the limited book-stores-plus-mailing-list mentality and are repackaging books as audiotapes.

If you are selling your product through one channel or perhaps two, your company is a troglodyte. Come outside and smell the roses. *There are several dozen channels that can generate cash-flow streams for you,* and the cost to open up these channels is minimal.

You are going to enter what may be a new space in your mental storage unit. You may think some of these ideas are slightly off the wall and perhaps untested. But somebody is using these strategies right now, and they are working. Therefore, if you step into one or two of them, you will not be like the pioneer who gets only arrows in his or her back. Furthermore, by multiplying your marketing channels you are making gatekeeper moves that will cause people—people you never thought you would earn a nickel on—to pay your company tolls for the right to sell to your customers (and non-customers).

Using Your Company Headline for Channeling

What does your fax paper have as a headline? Most likely, your company's name, address, telephone number, fax number, and three or four underlines to handwrite in the date, addressee, name of sender, and billing code.

Even if you go to half-sheet fax paper to halve the cost of each faxed page, there is still room at the bottom for a message about your product or service. Since the purpose of faxing something is to meet the need for instant communication, the headline (or footline, since it should properly come at the bottom of the fax cover sheet) should be current, up-to-date, and continually changing. A bright recruit in your marketing department can change the message every week. Here is my idea for a headline for an insurance product for a week in November:

This Week's Reasons to Buy Key Person Life Insurance:

NYT headline 11/16/92:	UTILITY EXECUTIVE KIDNAPPED
WSJ Page One 11/17/92:	MORE CORPORATE OFFICERS USE BODYGUARDS
CNN Reports 11/18/93:	NO CURE FOR PROSTATE CANCER IN SIGHT

If you manufacture packaging equipment, here's a possible headline for a week in November:

This Week's Reasons for Buying Jones Packaging Equipment:

Industry Week story 11/16/93:	STUDY SHOWS BLISTER-PACKED TOOLS SELL BETTER
Food Packaging headline 11/12/93:	FDA CRACKS DOWN ON POORLY PACKAGED CHEESES
Pravda headline 11/18/93:	U.S./RUSSIAN BORSCHT JOINT VENTURE WILL SPECIFY JONES PACKAGING EQUIPMENT

It may not create a sale. It may not even generate a solid prospect. But marketing headlines on your fax cover sheets bespeak an alert, aggressive company.

How's Your Stationery?

Take a look at your company's stationery. When was the last time you changed it? There is plenty of room on your stationery to put a headline about your mission statement (what you stand for). The bottom of the page is a logical place to make an important statement. Alternatively, you can write your complete mission statement in small print along the left side from top to bottom.

If putting your credo or mission statement on your stationery is too soppy, then print a smaller statement, such as "We support the Special Olympics with our profits."

Using Stocking-Stuffer Programs

You know how I feel about the company's envelope from the discussion about converting the mailroom to a profit center in Chapter 2. The envelope is shelf space. The U.S. Postal Service charges you a minimum of 29 cents a letter, so you should stuff your mailings with as much marketing propaganda—yours or your clients'—as you can.

In this chapter, however, I want to persuade you to "rent" space in another company's monthly statement. If your product or service is a consumer item that is priced to sell for between $60.00 and $120.00 per unit, it is an excellent candidate for an insert into the mailing envelopes of one of the following companies or services:

Sears, Roebuck	Nordstrom (or any department store)
J. C. Penney	Montgomery Ward
VISA	Monthly cable bill
MasterCard	Monthly pay life insurance
American Express	Automobile loan reminder

This idea is not breaking new marketing ground. Montgomery Ward offers prepaid legal insurance in its monthly statements and picks up an override on one of the fastest growing segments of American life—litigation.

But what are you doing with your product or service that a Sears or J. C. Penney customer might wish to know about? Do you accept payment via VISA or MasterCard? Your product advertisement or service message can tumble out of tens of millions of monthly statements of people who use VISA or MasterCard, selected by demographics or according to region of the country. *Yet the cost to you is printing and graphics only.* The owner of the envelope pays for postage and handling and keeps 20 to 25% of the price of the product or service. The statement stuffer consultant holds onto 5 to 10% for his or her effort.

Let's say your business is the marketing of Southwestern food and culinary items. You sell by catalog and through concessions in airport and travel-related gift shops. Your products cost from $10.00 to $150.00 and include cookbooks, barbecue utensils, aprons, mitts, frying pans, and your famous brand of Texas barbecue sauce sold in a six-pack like beer, but Texas-size. Your sales are $3.5 million per year, and you earn a gross profit margin of 50%. You give the concessionaires 33% and the catalog company, 33% as well. Therefore, before rent, utilities, telephone, travel, and salaries, your company is cash-flowing $577,500, which is distributed as follows:

Contribution to overhead	$577,500
Overhead:	
Office salaries	100,000
Personnel, benefits, FICA, insurance	25,000
Advertising	75,000
Rent	25,000
Telephone, fax machine	25,000
Postage, couriers	36,000
Travel	20,000
Insurance	6,000
Utilities	7,200
Professional fees	40,000
Dues, subscriptions	6,000
Total overhead	294,200
Balance to owner	$283,300

You have been earning about $283,300 each year for the last three years, but working 2,500 hours a year to achieve it. Let's put someone else's shelf space to work for you. Someone who charges 30% and gives you 70%.

You call American Express, let's say, or your statement stuffer consultant does, and ask to go into all of its monthly credit-card mailers to cardholders who bought an item in Texas in the last six months, preferably at a Texas retail store or hotel gift shop. American Express will know this information by zip code. You print some brochures—front and back—at a cost of $2,500, test them on 5,000 American Express cardholders, and generate a 1.5% presence—75 orders at $100 per order, or $7,500. You keep 70%, or $5,250, and roll that into a 2.5 million-piece printing.

This second mailing generates a 1.5% response, as well, or 37,500 orders at $100 per order. You have doubled the size of your company to $7.75 million—but look at the increase in cash flow, illustrated in Exhibit 17-1.

You have tripled your net cash flow by a statement-stuffer program using one new channel. You can expand the concept to many monthly billing envelopes.

Remember to store the names and addresses of your new customers in your computer. They are worth at least $1 per name—net, not gross.

Using Bounceback Cards

When a customer buys your product, do you capture his or her name and address? You should, because without a customer list you are reaching that customer one time, and perhaps only one time, and that is *not* constructing a highway with a tollgate on it. The traditional ways of capturing customer names and addresses is from credit-card receipts or warranty cards.

The most inexpensive way to develop a customer list is to insert a small index card or postcard in your packaging asking that the customer fill in his or her name and address (if you can capture age, telephone number, and location of the purchase, all the better). To induce the customer to take a moment to fill in the bounceback and to mail it back to you, you will have to invite the customer to do one of the three things the American consumer likes best:

1. Join a club.
2. Play a game.
3. Earn a discount.

Exhibit 17-1. Incremental cash flow from statement-stuffer program.

Net Sales—70% × $3.75 MM	$2,625,000
Less: Cost of sales	1,875,000
	750,000
Less: Printing	25,000
Net to incremental overhead	725,000
Less: 15 additional people to handle the orders at	
$5,000 each (for a one-month period)	75,000
Net additional cash flow	$ 650,000

Thus, your headline should say one of the following things (you can vary them to see which headline captures the largest number of filled-in bounceback cards):

1. "Join the ABC Picture Frame Company Happy Shopper's Club, where 10 purchases in one year entitles you to. . . ."
2. "How many words can you make up from the letters that spell our name, ABC Picture Frame Company? The winner receives an all-expense-paid trip to. . . . Second place wins. . . . Third place wins. . . . Entries must be in by December 31, 1993. Void if not permitted by state laws."
3. "Earn a 20% discount on your next purchase of ABC frames ordered through our catalog. Send for free catalog now."

It is just that simple to capture the names of your customers.

But, you protest, you make jam, or you produce celery. How do you fit a bounceback card the size of a postcard on a food item? You will have to design a label with the bounceback on the reverse side or pay supermarket store managers to have their checkout clerks ask customers to fill out bounceback cards during the checkout procedure. J. M. Smucker, the jelly and jam producer, pays store managers to capture the names and addresses of people who buy jelly and jams other than Smucker's in certain markets. Then it mails them a free sample of Smucker's jams. We'll have more on capturing the names of noncustomers later.

Affinity Group Marketing

"America is a nation of joiners." This observation was made not by Sol Price, the founder of The Price Clubs, or by the founder of Club Med, or by an entrepreneur who has created wealth by persuading Americans to join a club and pay a membership or subscription fee. The statement was made by a young Frenchman, Alexis de Tocqueville, in 1833, in his book *Democracy in America*.[1]

We Americans like to join clubs. We like to be part of groups that stand for something or have buying or voting power or have access to tee times, tennis court usage, or the town's softball fields. Such clubs are referred to in marketing circles as *affinity groups*, which are the basis for a new marketing strategy known as *affinity group marketing* (see Chapter 19). In its basic form, it assumes that if you control an affinity group—a club, association, league, or group—you can bargain with a provider of goods or services either to make its goods or services (or those of another organization with which it has a barter arrangement) available to the group's members at a discount or with a cash bonus payment or to offer them prizes, premiums, gifts, or special awards. Affinity group marketing is clearly apparent when you receive a mailing (or a telemarketing call) from your university alumni association suggesting that you take a cruise in the Caribbean, switch long-distance carriers, or buy an annuity. There is a punch line: Your alumni association will receive a generous gift from the cruise operator, the long-distance carrier, or the annuity issuer. From the point of view of the marketer of goods and services, the more individuals that it can convert to loyal (read "repeat") customers, the greater its sales. If it can leverage the loyalty of the individuals to their associations, clubs, leagues, or groups, then the sale is more easily (read "less expensively") made. It costs the association a mere endorsement and rewards the association (or its members directly) with cash, discounts, bonuses, prizes, premiums, gifts, and awards, or some of each.

Users Groups

The club concept is transferable to industrial products via the users group. The first users group expo I attended, organized by Hewlett-Packard, was held in a hotel conference room in Santa Barbara, California. The format has not changed, but the addition of gate-keeper features by user-group entrepreneurs over time has made users groups into an important marketing channel. Here's how they work.

Let's say that you make an industrial product that is sold, at a price of approximately $5,000 to $10,000, to several different industries and that there is a whole host of attachments, components, and software made by others that make the industrial product able to meet the specific needs of each industry. The personal computer or computer workstation fits this model, as do process control machines, compressors, conveyor equipment, tractors, and trucks.

The cash-flow channels that the users group provides, before you really roll up your sleeves and get creative, are shown in Exhibit 17-2.

Later we will add still more cash-flow channels. But just imagine selling 5,000 machines per year at $5,000 per machine, for gross revenues of $25 million and net cash flow of, say, $2.5 million before taxes, then adding $5.88 million on top of that, 90% of which goes straight to the bottom line, by selling the club concept to customers. And that's only the beginning. Here are the cash-flow components.

Exhibit 17-2. Cash-flow channels from the users group.

1. Assumptions:	
• Number of customers	5,000
• Number of users group meetings	2/year
• Number of suppliers of peripherals	100
2. Cash flow:	
a. Users group membership fee	
@ $1,000 per customer per year	$5,000,000
b. Exhibit space at users group expositions:	
• Peripheral suppliers at $500 per space × 2	200,000
• Service providers (25) at $5,000 per space × 2	250,000
c. Ads in users group magazine	
20 pages × $5,000 per page × 4 issues	400,000
d. Entrance fees (1,000 attendees at $15 ea. × 2)	30,000
Basic cash flow from users group	$5,880,000

• *Users group membership.* You as the manufacturer invite your customers to pay $1,000 up front, at the time of their purchase of your product, to join a "customers club," called a users group, the benefits of which are as follows:

- The users group will critique the product and provide advice and direction on improvements and refinements.
- The users group members will meet twice a year at users group expositions to provide their input and guidance to the manufacturer on new product development.
- The members will have a directory and receive a free monthly newsletter in which ideas from the members may be exchanged about the product's utility, expandability, and unique applications.
- The $1,000 contribution will be invested in new product development and innovations, to be shown first to the users groups members.

The users group membership is renewable, and if the particular product that unites the customers is subject to rapid technological change, most users eagerly renew. Plus, new users join the users group each time they make a purchase, which expands the cash flow year after year. If the manufacturer introduces new products or acquires companies that manufacture innovative new products, the customer bases for these products may represent spin-off user group opportunities, resulting in the manufacturer operating five, ten, or twenty users groups worth over $100 million per annum in net cash flow—a powerful series of tollgates in any industry.

• *Exhibit space.* Now the fun begins. You announce through the newsletter two users groups meetings per year: one in a Chicago hotel in the spring and the other in a Dallas hotel in the fall, at which symposiums will be held on the subjects of applications in several industries (one day), innovative peripheral product add-ons (one day), and recommendations for new product development (one day). The hotel's main conference room will be filled with booths rented by the manufacturers of components and software that operate on or with or add value to the sponsoring manufacturer's industrial machinery. These components and software producers are delighted to meet the end users, because their sales were made to aggregators and value-added resellers and they relish the opportunity to meet the end users to try to interest them in other add-ons. It is serious prospecting to a friendly audience. These components and software producers pay for booth space in advance, with the better spaces bringing higher prices.

• *Service provider space.* You will really clean up when you offer *industry-specific service provider space.* This means that one member of each of the primary services that would love to meet the exhibitors, your customers, and other attendees is given the opportunity to rent space, not in the exhibit hall, but in the hallways leading to it—on a first-come-first-served basis. The price is $5,000 to operate a booth for four days at the AB Compressor Corporation Users Group Exposition (ABCO-EX), and the following service groups compete fiercely for the space, permitting you to mark up the price each year to mind-boggling heights:

- Accounting firms
- Travel agencies
- Life insurance companies
- Property insurance companies
- Publishers (book)
- Publishers (magazine) several permitted)
- Banks
- Foreign governments' trade departments (several)
- Temporary-help agencies
- Executive search firms
- Engineering firms
- Appraisers
- Investment banking firms (several)
- Stock brokerages
- Equipment leasing companies
- Graphic design firms
- Advertising agencies

Note my warning to you in the Introduction: like the movie *Field of Dreams*, when the voice tells Kevin Costner's character "Build it. They will come." The same applies in gatekeeping. Build a highway to your customers, and others will pay you a toll to come meet them.

• *Ads in users group magazines*. What is a celebratory event without a magazine? Each users group has its "Show Daily." The magazine presells 20 to 100 pages of advertisements to booth renters, restaurants, and retail stores in the exposition city and others, puts in 30 to 50 pages of articles taken from the users group newsletters and other sources, and adds five pages on what to do and where to go while in town. Except for 20 pages of photographs of attendees and late-breaking stories—mergers, new product announcements, executive changes—which are produced on the first morning of the show, the magazine is printed at night and distributed free to attendees' hotel rooms and in lobby containers. Richard Ekstract, founder of Viare, invented the concept of the "Show Daily" for the Consumer Electronics Exposition and has produced them under contract for many expo promoters. He does not get much sleep during the shows, since the magazines are produced and delivered at night. In our cash-flow projection, I assume only two magazines per users group meeting, even though you could actually publish four per meeting, plus one per month during the year.

• *Entrance fees*. The general public will want to attend ABCO-EX if it is held in a city near their offices to see if any of the products shown could make their jobs easier or save them money. The entrance fee should be kept low because they are *noncustomers*, and users group meetings capture noncustomers. Remember, your booth will be the most attractive and best located of them all, with plenty of seats, hard candy, premiums, and smiling marketing staff members.

More Tolls to Collect

Once you have put on two or three users group meetings and gotten the hang of it, you can get into some serious multiple toll collecting. Here are some ideas. Pick the half-dozen that suit you and subcontract them to a division within your company that you later partially spin off to the public at a high p/e ratio as Exposition Planning and Service:

1. *The seal-of-approval business*. What better place to announce the formation of a trade group to set standards for the quality of goods and services sold to your customers than at your users group meet-

ings? A subsidiary of your company with a board of advisors made up of important customers can set the actual standards, your company will test new products and services for a fee, and you will advise the standards-setting committee. The fee can be based on the number of hours that your engineers spend studying the products; once approved, the components can be stamped ABCO-APPROVED.

The side purposes of a standards-setting association are usually more interesting than the toll collecting. I was with Frank Lautenberg, then the president of Automatic Data Processing and later elected a senator from New Jersey, the night he dreamed up ADAPSO—the Association of Data Processing Service Organizations—the standard-setting association for the U.S. software industry. Lautenberg was frustrated at the travel and due-diligence cost of acquiring software companies for ADP. He thought up ADAPSO as a way to bring the targets to him in New Jersey.

At the first meeting of ADAPSO, Lautenberg and the other members of the newly formed organization introduced themselves. Suddenly, napkins were passed along from person to person. The napkins had financial statements written on them, along with the name of the company and the owner's name, hotel, and room number. ADP made three quick and successful acquisitions the first year of ADAPSO's existence.

Earning fees for setting standards is not new by any means. The Better Homes & Gardens Seal of Approval has been a highly valued endorsement throughout most of the twentieth century.

2. *Symposium proceedings.* Some customers who are unable to attend the users group meeting may be keenly interested in learning what was discussed in the technical meetings. Accordingly, the sponsoring manufacturer should tape the proceedings and make them available both in print and on audiocassette. The proceedings must not be made too expensive for users group members, but they can bring in about $10.00 to $12.00 per day's proceedings when sold to new customers. This marketing channel is known as the information channel.

3. *The travel business.* After you have sponsored one or two users group meetings, you will have a fairly good idea of the head count, where members come from, and how long they stay. For a $5,000 up-front fee, your company can form a travel agency and earn a 15% fee by booking rooms and airplane seats for attendees of the users group meetings. Better yet, your company can rent several thousand seats and beds at a steep discount and resell them to attendees.

Senior Expos

My idea of a new marketing channel for producers of pharmaceuticals or healthy foods that appeal to people above 50 years of age is the Senior Expo: a users group for senior citizens held in 50 venues across the country at the rate of one per week. Service industries, franchising companies, insurers, health care providers, publishers—the number of potential booth space renters reaches into the hundreds. The first company to recognize seniors with their very own expositions would represent a significant new cash-flow channel for a pharmaceutical, health and beauty aids, or food producer.

Other User Groups

Other expos leap to mind, along with their ancillary cash-flow channels. Manufacturers of fitness equipment could profit from this marketing channel multiplier. City people who buy country property represent yet another untapped users group, perhaps for manufacturers of tractors. Producers of telecommunications equipment represent another users group opportunity, one that health insurance products could tap into.

Competing With Yourself: Anything Worth Doing Is Worth Replicating

If your product is good, if it works, if it solves the customers' problems, it will attract competitors who will come at you at the lower end of the qualify spectrum.

It is important, therefore, to compete with yourself: to bring out a low-end replication of your successful product. On the face of it, it might seem strange to set up the situation where you, as a manufacturer, compete with yourself. But it actually makes sense. Here are three reasons:

1. You deny the opportunity to a competitor.
2. You put more production through your plant, which means spreading overhead and increasing profits.
3. You can direct product through other channels and find *non-customers*—consumers who currently do not buy from you—who then become your company's customers.

Using Private Labeling to Reach Noncustomers

Approximately 60 to 85% of the consumers in your marketplace do not buy your products. Again, they are even more important to your company than your customers are because there are more of them and because they are where your growth will come from. You can try to reach them through advertising, which is expensive, or you can sell to a tollgate operator who controls access to that market and let the tollgate operator spend the advertising dollars to reach them. Obviously, it makes sense to sell to the tollgate operator. The marginal profits to be derived from producing 10% more products at a lower gross profit margin could make the difference between a good year and a terrific year.

An Example of Private Labeling

Assume that you manufacture a product with a 45% gross profit margin, a 5% ratio of advertising to sales, and a 10% ratio of selling expenses to sales. Further, assume that the company has sales of $20 million per year with its branded line and general and administrative expenses of $2.2 million per year.

The company agrees to manufacture a version of its product line for a customer that will put its own label on the product and sell it alongside your product in its stores. The private label price is at 50% gross profit margin. The customer orders $4 million of products. The effect on your company's bottom line is shown in Exhibit 17-3.

In this example, the company experiences a 20% increase in sales, which translates into a 56% increase in profits. Its general and administrative expenses increase to accommodate the additional expenses of adding a partial shift. Its plant is more productive, and its cash flow is enriched by $1.8 million by the mere act of competing with itself. But what I like best of all is that the company captures noncustomers and makes them customers. The noncustomers previously belonged to a competitor. Private labeling is leveraging the tollgate operator.

Making Private Labeling Succeed

As with any marketing strategy, the first step in using private labeling is to conduct consumer research. Determine the importance of branded merchandise in the marketplace. Is it greater or less than the brand name of the retailer or reseller who carries your company's brand? Will the reseller promote the private-label brand heavily or

Exhibit 17-3. The profitability of private labeling.

Annual Operating Statement

	Before Private Labeling		After Private Labeling	
	%	($000s)	%	($000s)
Revenues	100.0	$20,000	100.0	$24,000
Cost of goods sold	55.0	11,000	54.1	13,000
Gross profit	45.0	9,000	45.9	11,000
Selling expenses	10.0	2,000	8.3	2,000
Advertising expenses	5.0	1,000	4.2	1,000
General & administrative expenses	11.0	2,200	10.0	2,400
Total operating expenses	26.0	5,200	22.5	5,400
Net operating income	19.0	3,800	23.3	5,600
Interest expense	3.0	600	2.5	600
Net profit before taxes	16.0	$ 3,200	20.8	$ 5,000

merely put it on the shelf and hope that consumers will select it? Packaging is central to sales of private-label merchandise, primarily to avoid the appearance of a second-rate product. In fact, private-label products should be packaged to appear upscale but priced in mid-range. In women's apparel, The Limited women's clothing lines have done an exemplary job with private labeling.

Upscale private labels give retailers and reseller the opportunity to market a line on a basis other than price.

An Example of Private-Labeling Success: A&P's Master Choice and Western Family Foods

A&P has created a loyal customer base for its Master Choice line of foods, private-labeled for it by Western Family Foods in Portland, Oregon. A&P advertises the brand under the slogan "It Only Tastes Expensive."

"We saw the opportunity to fill the gap between national brands and gourmet foods," says Charles E. Calbom, president of Western Family. Master Choice products are sold within 10% of the retail price of the leading national brand and 50% below similar gourmet items.

Western Family and A&P have achieved their greatest success when they go up against regional brands, rather than heavily advertised national brands. Two Master Choice winners are frozen pizza and ice cream. Peter O'Gorman, senior vice president for development and marketing for A&P, said that A&P and Western Family worked together for nine months to develop a private-label ice cream that they believed was superior to Ben & Jerry's, the industry upscale benchmark.

Note

1. Alexis de Tocqueville, *Democracy in America*, ed. J. P. May and M. Lerner (New York: Dell, 1966).

18

Locating Noncustomers

There is no single means of multiplying your company's cash flow better than locating your company's noncustomers and making them your customers. This process is inexpensive, very inexpensive, if you select an elegant solution and stop wasting money on advertising. The elegant solution is something I call the information solution.

The Information Solution

Think of the market for your products or services as a pyramid. The market share you control is at the top. It's small. Your noncustomers are at the base of the pyramid. In the middle are alliances, networks, licensees, competitors, some customers, and some noncustomers—as many as 20 new sources of cash flow that you can reach with multiple distribution channels. (See Exhibit 18-1.)

The gatekeeper marketing strategy is to fill the middle of the pyramid with many new cash-flow sources, thereby driving noncustomers into the top layer. When the noncustomer becomes first the customer and then a renewable customer—i.e., an annuity—and buys multiple products from your company on an ongoing basis, the pyramid changes shape at the top to become a square, and you have achieved profound leverage.

Pyramiding Users Groups

Let's assume you own a pharmaceutical company. Assume, too, that one of your entrepreneurial managers—let's say it's your human resources officer—has some solutions for the problem of drug and chemical dependency among your corporate executives. Concerned about the human suffering caused by drug and chemical depen-

Exhibit 18-1. A model of your market.

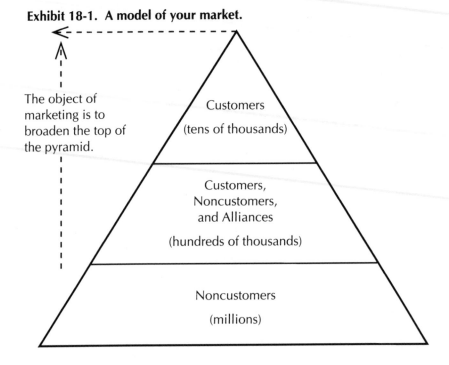

The object of marketing is to broaden the top of the pyramid.

Customers
(tens of thousands)

Customers,
Noncustomers,
and Alliances

(hundreds of thousands)

Noncustomers

(millions)

dency, the human resources officer suggests to you that the families receive counseling.

You grant the human resources officer permission to do family counseling with employees to explore some ways to handle the problem. She becomes experienced in the field and begins to make progress within the company, making you and your senior management more sensitive to this issue. You agree that she can publish a newsletter to be mailed to other corporate human resources officers as long as the newsletter is tied into creating more sales for your company's pharmaceuticals.

Building the Marketing Pyramid

The human resources officer begins the new endeavor by sketching a pyramid of the market (see Exhibit 18-2). Her object is to convert as many of the 2,000 human resources officers as possible into clients, to widen the pyramid at the top by making the market aware of the problem.

Exhibit 18-2. Market pyramid for corporate consulting business.

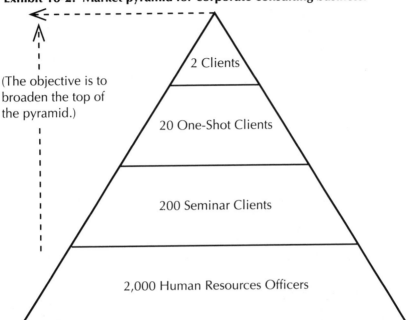

(The objective is to broaden the top of the pyramid.)

2 Clients

20 One-Shot Clients

200 Seminar Clients

2,000 Human Resources Officers

Newsletter Start-Up

Many entrepreneurs have begun business with a newsletter. It is a unique means of customer financing. The human resources officer's corporate chemical dependency newsletter is offered to 2,000 other human resources officers on a subscription basis, 10 issues for $120. If 400 people subscribe, your human resources officer has $48,000 in launch capital. It is possible to attract advertisers for a newsletter, but this particular newsletter does not immediately suggest any potential ads.

Seminar Marketing

In the first two or three months she publishes the newsletter, your human resources officer reports on her subject from every vantage point imaginable: the human angle, the legal angle, the moral angle, and so on. In the fourth month, believing that some of the subscribers are ready to discuss the issue, she announces a seminar. For $500 each the human resources officers can meet in Chicago for two days of panel discussion and lectures by psychologists and psychiatrists. Checks are received from 75 human resources officers, yielding $37,500 in revenues. Your human resources officer spends $10,000 on a first-class seminar—good lunches, interesting speakers, and a comfortable hotel (the guests pay for lodging). She makes back her $10,000 in costs by selling tapes of the seminar to nonattendees for $75 each.

Growth of Dependency Counseling Business

Through the seminar your human resources officer gets leads from 75 corporate officers who are beginning to understand the extent of their problem. She offers each of them a small consulting assignment: one day's analysis for $1,000. Twenty corporations sign up over the next three months, providing further revenues of $20,000.

From these 20 consulting assignments the officer is awarded two performance contracts. She will counsel all families that are suffering from the chemical dependence problem and assess for the client corporation the likelihood that they can recover, given treatment. The contracts are each worth $25,000 plus expenses for one year. Thus, after the first 12 months of operation, your human resources officer has generated the following revenues:

Performance contracts	$ 50,000
Consulting assignments	20,000
Seminars, tapes	47,500
Newsletter	48,000
Total Revenues	$165,000

In the second year, the newsletter might double its revenues. There could be two seminars, one on each coast, another 20 consulting assignments, and four new performance contracts. As revenues approach $300,000, your human resources officer is able to hire a staffer to publish the newsletter, assist with the seminars, and keep the books.

Entering the third year, you might add another human resources officer to the company. Your human resources officer will find other ways to permit growth of revenues, such as issuing books and videos, without sacrificing quality.

The pyramid method for tackling a new market that needs to be more problem-aware is an entrepreneurial creation. Your pharmaceutical sales grow as information about your products spreads. But you have also created a new profit center, a new cash flow channel: the information division. Look at its value: net cash flow of $300,000 after two years times a p/e ratio of 15 translates into an additional $4.5 million in value.

Translating the Information Channel into a Spin-Off

Once you have built up the information channel so that it, along with your more conventional product and service sales, is pumping cash flow, you can spin off partial ownership of the human resources company and put $1.5 million or more of cash in your pocket. Masco Industries just did this with several subsidiaries.

Progressive Corporation's Information Channel

Proposition 103, passed by angry California voters in 1988, both set limits on the profits of companies that sold insurance in the state and called for a rollback of insurance rates. As a result, many insurers pulled out of California and others became less aggressive marketers, leaving only a small number of companies offering auto insurance, and at widely varying rates.

Peter B. Lewis, the founder and CEO of Progressive Corporation, a Cleveland underwriter of substandard auto insurance and motorcycle insurance, saw the handwriting on the wall. Progressive could no longer make a decent profit in California, but it had sunk costs there. Pulling out was out of the question, and no one would buy Progressive's book of California insurance.

So Lewis entered the information business with a new service called Express Quote, which helps consumers compare auto insurance rates quickly. Customers call a toll-free number and are interviewed for approximately 10 minutes about details that affect rates, such as age, driving record, and make and model of car. For $25, Progressive will send callers a list of auto insurance rates from the eight largest auto insurers in California, all tailored to the customer's specifications.

As a smart tollgate operator, Progressive is offering to include insurance carriers other than the top eight that want to reach Express Quote's customers. If the venture succeeds in California, Lewis may roll it out to other states. In time, he intends to broaden the amount of information given the consumer to include the number of complaints filed against each insurer with the state insurance commissioners.

Putting a Microchip at the Cash Register

Strategic Information Systems, or SIS, an entrepreneurial company in Hartford, Connecticut, rents space in pharmacies at the cash register. It places an interactive video with a satellite uplink in the back of the store that permits SIS's subscribers—pharmaceutical and health and beauty aids producers—to communicate with noncustomers at the time they purchase a competitor's product. For example, a purchaser of Ban deodorant can interact with Bristol-Myers, the producer of Sure deodorant, via a touchtone screen. Bristol-Myers's noncustomer will be asked several questions about why he or she likes Ban and does not like Sure. Demographic information on the noncustomer can be collected, as well. Moreover, Bristol-Myers can offer the noncustomer a free sample of Sure.

If this interaction occurs several thousand times a day at locations throughout the country, the subscribers to SIS can gain a stunning amount of information about its noncustomers in a very short period of time and reposition its products accordingly. SIS charges its subscribers less than $40,000 per year for the service.

Direct Response Marketing

Tradition-bound companies continue to spend 5 to 10% of their revenues on television and print advertisements. In 1991, advertising expenditures on television were approximately $34 billion, up from $12.3 billion in 1983, even as consumers cut back the number of hours spent in front of the tube. Similar readership declines exist for newspaper, the nation's second largest advertising media.

Increasingly, however, advertisers are shunning television and print media and spending their money on nontraditional advertising strategies. One of these is direct response marketing.

The Basics of Direct Response Marketing

The first step in direct response marketing is to rent several lists of names of consumers who buy products or services similar to yours via the mail. You can rent these lists from list brokers and test various lists by sending the same mailer to a random selection of names drawn from each of the lists, and evaluating the response rates. You can then apply a similar procedure to telemarketing.

In your trials, the mailer (or caller) can describe the product or service and then ask for the order and/or provide a bounceback ("Send for our free catalog" or "To request more information, send for . . ."). The direct-response message, along with an 800 number, can also be placed in a newspaper or magazine or on television or radio.

By first delivering the same message to a variety of lists or media and then using the lists (or media) that produce the best results to test variations of the message, you can learn which consumers respond to which version of the message, thereby minimizing your reliance on subjective judgments. In the meantime, you are creating a large list of generically interested nonconsumers (people who request the catalog or product information but who are not buyers).

Obtaining and Using Brokers' Lists

Names on a broker's list rent for 5 to 10 cents each. If the names have ordered a product by mail order within the last ninety days and have paid more than $100 for the item, they are worth closer to 10 cents each; the cheaper names have purchased the product via mail order within the last 12 months but have paid less for it. Further, the older the list, the lower its value because of obsolescence—consumers move, and their circumstances change. It is better to spend a few cents more per name and rent a fresher list. By the way, list brokers usually require a minimum order of from 3,000 to 5,000 names.

Lists are rented on Cheshire label or on computer printer paper, depending on the vendor's preference. You can eliminate duplicate names and avoid sending several mailers to the same address by having a list management firm do a merge-purge-dupe-drop run through its computer.

To test five separate lists, each containing 20,000 names (and applying the reduced postage costs that we discussed in Chapter 2), your costs would be as follows:

100,000 × .074 (a)	=	$ 7,500
100,000 × .11	=	11,000
Presort costs	=	2,000
Stationery costs	=	3,000
Copywriting, design, production of mailer	=	7,000
Total		$30,500

(a) The average of $.05 and $.10 per name lists

This is roughly the equivalent of buying one-quarter of a page in a popular national monthly magazine (plus a 15% advertising agency fee). Assume that the five lists produce a .5% response (500 orders) for a $100 product, or $50,000 in sales. If your cost of goods sold is less than $19,500 (39% of sales), you will recoup your $30,500 investment in cash and can test more lists or resolicit the list with the highest response rate.

A direct-response mailer such as the one described here might generate a 3% response, or revenues of $300,000. The leverage on $30,500 is $300,000/$30,500 = 9.8. The larger the response, the higher the leverage.

Telemarketing is the oral equivalent of a direct-response mailing piece. A trained caller with a script calls names from a list selected because it has produced interest in the consumer's generic area in the past. Telemarketing is superior to direct-response mailing because the caller can ask and obtain responses to dozens of questions, whereas the direct-response mailer can only ask the respondent to order or to request information about the product or service. The more expensive the consumer product—cars, tractors, homes, recreational vehicles—the more affordable telemarketing becomes.

Among the more compelling reasons to use direct-response mailing and telemarketing is that they permit you to acquire a great deal of information about your consumers and nonconsumers. Traditional advertising lacks this feedback feature and also lacks the immediacy of the sale.

Artificial Intelligence as Marketing Support

If you begin utilizing direct-response marketing and telemarketing (with computer assistance) to lower costs and speed up data messaging, then you will begin to learn, in some detail, who your customers are and what their preferences are. And you will begin to gain the leverage that comes from having that information. Some of the most fascinating developments in consumer testing are going on, not in advertising agencies, but in computer software firms. When the power of these techniques is felt in large consumer products companies, advertising agencies that have not adopted them as their primary research tool will need to catch up in a hurry. Looking ahead to the next decade, I foresee a rapid downsizing of the advertising industry and a rise in artificial intelligence-based telemarketing.

Several companies have begun to use artificial intelligence, or A-I, to test consumer response to products and services and to determine what factors determine why a consumer buys a certain product and why he or she will or will not repurchase the product at a future date. The value of A-I in the test phase of consumer research is that the computer can both analyze large amounts of data very rapidly and identify trends, creating "decision trees" that help researchers develop follow-up questions and interpret the data. From thousands of interviews the A-I software researcher can pluck the responses that show that certain car owners relate to certain key words. "Look at the relationship," says the A-I software. "Mercedes-Benz owners used the word engineering an average of five times during the interview."

You might wish to investigate A-I software packages that are applicable to consumer research. But A-I is only as good as the telemarketing script.

Lexi: An Example of the Leverage of Customer Information

Robin Richards, CEO of Lexi International of Los Angeles, operates an A-I-based telemarketing consumer research company that tests products for nationally branded consumer marketing companies. Lexi has delivered sales increases of more than 400% for some of its clients, while reducing their advertising expenditures. Lexi cut the advertising budget of one dealer in European luxury cars from $500 per car sale to $375, and increased the dealer's sales on some weekends from 5 to 20 cars.

Lexi uses A-I to generate a substantial amount of background data on consumers before the telemarketer is given their names and addresses. By accessing publicly available data, the telemarketer knows the consumer's address and whether he or she owns a house, whether it has a pool, whether it backs up on a golf or tennis club, plus the make, model, and year of the consumer's car (from which a trade-in price can be established). The telemarketer can engage the consumer in conversation at any number of levels, and the computer can match responses against a personality characteristics grid. The telemarketer can close with a trade-in offer on the consumer's car and a special invitation to visit the showroom.

The invitation (the direct-response mailer) is an engraved card with the consumer's name done in calligraphic style. The response rate to the special invitation has run as high as 80%, and the close rate in the dealer's showroom is equally high, owing to the deep segmentation and prequalification made possible by A-I.

Lexi charges its customers less than the amount they would typically spend on a month's advertising to sell 40 cars. With Lexi managing their marketing, the dealers each sell more than 120 cars per month, allowing them a handsome profit. The Lexi system works for a wide array of consumer products—bank loans, home sales, consumer electronics, personal computer systems—as well as for industrial products and financial services.

Communicating to Turn Noncustomers into Customers

Every other month I receive a magazine published by General Electric Capital Corporation, the financial services subsidiary of GE, which is the consummate raider-managed company. Although I may never bring a leveraged buyout to GE Capital, because its criteria and my deal flow may not fit, you can be sure that I know that GE Capital wants my business. Although I am GE Capital's noncustomer today, I just may be its customer tomorrow, so it's willing to spend $5 every other month to give me an interesting newsletter.

Coopers & Lybrand, the public accounting firm, does the same thing with its interesting monthly newsletter, which is filled with tax and audit tips and with interpretations of government rulings that affect businesses. This newsletter is sent to scores of client leads in an effort to turn noncustomers into customers. The other major accounting firms also publish interesting newsletters. One, Ernst & Young, sponsors seminars and invites entrepreneurs to speak to venture capitalists, in a different effort to turn noncustomers into new clients. Law firms also do this; Boyer & Norton, a Houston law firm that specializes in lender liability lawsuits, publishes a monthly newsletter that is disseminated to nonclients.

The lesson in all of this is that, by making contact as few as six times per year, you can accomplish three things:

1. You remind noncustomers that you still want to be their provider of products or services.
2. You demonstrate that service is a mainstay of your business.
3. You keep your mailing list up-to-date.

19

Affinity Group Marketing

"The flowers had the look of flowers that were looked at" has long been my favorite line from T. S. Eliot. At the risk of commercializing this giant of poetry, don't we all want our products to have the look of products that are looked at? But colorful fields of flowers are all over the place; that is one reason poets can rhapsodize about them. Unfortunately, our products (and services) are limited as to their ubiquitousness.

We can change that by competing less and cooperating more. That sounds heretical, doesn't it? Government has persuaded us that competition is good and cooperation is prima facie bad. The Sherman Antitrust Act makes it illegal in many instances to cooperate with competitors. That knocks out the tremendous benefits of shared research and development costs, training costs, and manufacturing facilities.

However, we are still able to cooperate with noncompetitors. This practice, called affinity marketing, has become so popular that it is the zeitgeist of marketing strategies of the 1990s. Its origins are in the Law of Reciprocity, which governs all commerce.

Simply stated, the Law of Reciprocity describes mutual trust. For instance, you and I can agree to a deal in which you trust me to deliver something of value and I trust you to deliver payment for the item I deliver. If you default, I will default. But as long as you cooperate, I will continue cooperating.

In affinity group marketing, I persuade you not to pay me for the valuable product or service that I will deliver. Instead, you allow me access to your customers, your channel, your airwaves, your members, your subscribers, your shelf spaces, or some other commodity. Your customers will receive value, but you will actually pay nothing.

The value to me is that I persuade you to raise your tollgate without charging an up-front fee. The payment you eventually receive (or the savings you eventually achieve) is backend-weighted and derives from my sale of something to your customers.

Cooperating with Other Companies for Mutual Profit

I bought a top-of-the-line Xerox copier a few months ago. When the salesman asked me for the order, I asked, "What is your affinity deal?" The salesman said, "You will get the Xerox preferred customer rate given us by Airborne Express." Because Airborne's preferred customer rate was lower than the rate we were paying our existing overnight courier, we switched. Airborne didn't have to spend a penny to get my company as a new customer.

If you want other companies to use their sales forces, their selling space, their mailers, and their capital to locate noncustomers for your company, then offer them an affinity group marketing deal. Have their customers become your customers by offering the companies the right to toss in the privilege of purchasing your product or service each time customers purchase theirs.

Developing Tie-Ins

Whom do you go to to develop tie-ins, or affinity relationships? There are consultants who specialize in developing tie-ins, but if you put your mind to it, you can let your fingers do the walking through your industry's trade journals and through lists of subscribers to Dun & Bradstreet and its *Million-Dollar Directory* or *Thomas Register.*

One industry that is actively looking for tie-ins is the automobile industry. For instance, consider the deal between General Motors and MasterCard to offer a new credit card that offers credits on GM cars. Virtually every industrial company is seeking customers with the fervor of a rookie IRS agent ferreting out tax cheats. Here are some possible affinity deals for you to consider:

Your Company	*Affinity Candidates*
1. Oil-field products sold to emerging democracies	Travel discounts on foreign carriers
2. Sports equipment manufacturers	Discounts on fitness center memberships
3. Life insurance	Discounts on pharmaceuticals
4. Office equipment	Discounts on companion products, paper, supplies, pens

| 5. Food products | Discounts at stores in shop-ping center |

The U.S. Postal Service could make a fortune with affinity group marketing, but it would offend the purists. Coca-Cola, Pepsico, Gatorade, Delta Airlines, and hundreds of consumer products and service marketers would love to buy a few centimeters on postage stamps. Federal Express has plenty of room on its packages to rent a patch of affinity space. Coca-Cola could put messages on its cans that tie in with another product or service.

Why do we compete constantly when there are so many opportunities to be taken advantage of by cooperating?

Marketing by Association Endorsement

Painters and sculptors are a class of dealmakers that has long used third-party endorsements in order to sell its product. The endorsers are the lists of museums and well-known collectors who have purchased the artists' works; these lists appear in publications about the artists. Important painters and sculptors have long sought patrons who will donate their work to art museums, thus providing the artists with the endorsement necessary to sell more art at higher and higher prices. Collectors are eager to donate art to museums, both for tax purposes and to achieve the privileges and social acclaim that accompany generous gifts to museums. As Will and Ariel Durant have written, giving art to museums is a means of "perfuming one's fortune."

The artists of the Renaissance, who cultivated wealthy patrons like the Medici, were the founders of the strategy of third-party endorsement via an association. The strategy is simplicity itself: After formulating your concept or solution, create an association in the form of a not-for-profit organization and have the association set standards for the concept; these standards encompass your product and possibly exclude others.

For instance, if you create a new process for fueling cars with the ethanol captured from landfills, immediately form the Association of Alternative Fuel Providers. Next step: Begin publishing its newsletter. Third step: Sponsor seminars to promote interest in alternative automobile fuels, and explain the benefits of your product. Note how the endorsement factor can roll into multichannel marketing: endorsement-to-association-to-newsletters-to-seminars-to-backtable product sales.

20

Air Space ("Free") Marketing

There are very few available real estate sites remaining in the United States. As any investor in commercial real estate will tell you, if you can hear him through his sobs, the country is overbuilt. *Barron's* estimates that some regions, such as Dallas and Los Angeles, have enough excess real estate on hand to carry them for 40 years.

This consideration makes the shelf and floor space of successful retailers very expensive. A few years ago supermarkets began charging food and health and beauty aids suppliers so-called slotting allowances, fees charged vendors of new products that are relatively untested for the privilege of putting the items on a supermarket's shelves. This applies to General Mills as well as to a start-up manufacturer of tofu-based pasta.

The search for product display space is so intense that shopping center landlords are selling retail space to restaurants and others in the far reaches of their parking lots.

But there is free space in the retail stores, if you are clever enough to have an advertiser pay you for a service that the retailer finds sufficiently interesting to bring into (or place in the front of) her store. Information products and services are popular air space marketers.

Pharmacies have determined that people waiting on line for their prescriptions to be filled want to know more about their illnesses. Medical Strategies, an early-stage company based in Boston, Massachusetts, places information kiosks in pharmacies that enable customers to read (on a screen or a printout) about their illnesses. A short ad trailer paid for by the pharmaceutical company that produces a relevant product follows the description. Wal-Mart and other pharmacies claim they sell more drugs in stores with kiosks than in those without.

Let's say you manufacture pump valves and fittings for the public utility industry and for water companies. You can copy the Medical Strategies idea by publishing a monthly newsletter for *all* of the employees of the public utilities and water companies to inform them about activities at other utilities, government issues, environmental issues, and personalities. Moreover, you can sell advertising space to allied companies in your newsletter. If you print and mail 1 million copies per month and sell five ad pages per issue at $25,000 per page, you have generated $1.5 million.

Air Space Marketers

Selling products and services in the aisles and near the checkout counters of retail chains is another way of leveraging the tollgate operators. In 1987 the business school at Northwestern University did a study of trends in supermarket selling practices that provides insight into the direction these stores are taking. Retailers want more fast-turning, high-profit-margin products that do not require capital investment. Freezers filled with food and refrigerators filled with soft drinks are not the direction of the future. Greeting cards, stationery, videos, impulse items, and take-out food will be displayed on racks in free real estate, and they will carry high profit margins.

ActMedia, a company that puts minibillboards on supermarket shopping carts, has changed the direction of point-of-sale (POS) marketing gambits from simple messages on shopping bags to electronic shopping carts that have audio and visual messages. In the point-of-sale business a tollgate operator agrees to "rent" aisle space, air space, and equipment to the POS company, which seeks to stimulate the sale of products or services by capturing the interest of the consumer when he or she is in a consuming frame of mind. The word "rent" is in quotes because the fee is frequently not fixed but rather a percentage of sales. If it is fixed, it is often very low. The tollgate operator—the retailer—is willing to open its valuable real estate to an air space marketer because that portion of its real estate is not generating revenues anyway and because the POS company can make a persuasive case for its ability to generate more ring-ups at the cash register.

ActMedia made the shopping cart an extremely valuable piece of real estate. But the significance of ActMedia to our approach to management is far greater. The search for air space and free real estate inside the tollgate can be compared with the California Gold Rush of 1849.

Why? Because there are very few undeveloped parcels of land in industrialized countries that are suitable for new shopping centers. This means little new shelf space. Little new shelf space means that consumer products marketers will have to become more imaginative in conceiving ways to introduce new products. Air space, including J-hooks, end-of-aisle buckets, bouncebacks, newsletters, and inserts in billing envelopes, will become standard. If marketers fail to become imaginative, their cash flows will head south.

What steps can you take to maximize cash flow? Grab and control as much air space as possible. Here are some strategies that you can implement today:

• *Hotel rooms.* The hotel television set is an example of air space that is attracting POS marketers. Producers of continuing legal education courses and similar programs have discovered it, and hotel and motel chain tollgate operators are delighted to have the lawyers, along with accountants and physicians, rent their rooms so they can meet their requirements for forty hours a year of mandatory training. But consumers need not be professionals to learn from television classrooms. Book and magazine publishers can put quite a bit of branded merchandise, such as instructional and business videos, on hotel television screens, sharpening the skills of business and student travelers.

• *Other Air Space Strategies.* Wherever there is a tollgate providing access to consumers, there exist air space selective leveraging opportunities. Airplanes represent excellent tollgates in which to market products, either in the aisles or at the end of the aisles. Travelers tend to be upscale, and many are at leisure, so you have plenty of time to rent audiocassettes and video games and to sell products.

Car washes are another example. They have air space in their waiting rooms, which represent opportunities to sell books on cassette, automotive supplies, greeting cards, and other items that can be displayed on racks. The more idle time the consumer spends at the tollgate, the greater the number of products that can be sold there.

Multiple Expos

Once you get the knack of sponsoring expos, the skill is transferable to foreign markets and to other markets that lack expositions or users groups. The *Trade Show Journal* lists all of the nation's trade shows.

You can steer clear of these, and operate expos for inventors, frequent travelers, and fitness, gardening, foods/cooking, and college-bound consumers.

Clutter

One of the things I like best about shopping at Wal-Mart or one of the wholesale clubs is the clutter. I like crowded aisles. I like narrow aisles stacked to the sky. At Kuhn's Hardware on Melrose Boulevard in Los Angeles, there are "double shelves" on some of the aisles. In addition to the stationary shelves stuffed with dozens of items, if you pull on a rope, you can lower to eye level a sheet of thin plywood that has yet more goods hung onto it via J-hooks. Instead of 20 aisles of hardware, Kuhn's has the equivalent of about 30 aisles, achieved through modular shelves (operated by the customer, hence no additional labor cost) and adding no rental or overhead costs. The pull-down shelves narrow the aisles further and add to the sense of clutter.

Consumers are tired of the antiseptic look. They know that to have neatness, orderliness, and organization, the retailer has to pay higher labor costs, which are passed on to consumers. But in factory-to-you-type stores, there are boxes strewn everywhere and end-of-aisle buckets and displays and dozens of racks guarding the checkout counters like tollgates. We bump into other carts like Dodgems (the electric cars that we rode as kids in the state fairs two or three decades ago). People seem friendlier and happier and in more of a buying mood in cluttered stores.

Flea Markets

Before you laugh off flea markets, check their average space rental price: around $10 for eight feet of selling space on weekends. J. C. Penney signs up more new credit card customers at flea markets than it does in its stores. Dwight Sample, manager of the J. C. Penney store in Winter Park, Florida, explains why: "People at flea markets are more at their leisure."

Long-distance telephone carriers, such as MCI and Sprint, also sign up more new customers at flea markets than they do via direct-mail marketing. Even marketers of high-end consumer products, such as Mercedes-Benz, have begun renting air space at flea markets.

Other Air Space Marketing Opportunities

I am in favor of having car washes offer me books on cassette via a rental library (that encourages me to return in a week) while I stand in their waiting rooms. I am interested in seeing business videos in my hotel room, and I will rent them for $10.00 an hour if they will help me in negotiating, selling, saying "no" more frequently, or becoming a better boss.

Airport terminals should have a section for flea markets, or at least for used-book stands. Their bookstores tend to carry a handful of best-sellers only. The Milwaukee airport had an excellent used-book store in it for many years. I would be willing to pay $3.00 to browse through an airport flea market or a quality used-book store while waiting for a delayed flight. Car rental company airport vans (which should be shared by the car rental companies to save money, which could be passed on to the customers) have a small amount of air space in which to do some tie-in marketing. When I rent a car in a distant city, I do not know which radio stations are suited to my taste in news, talk, or music. The car rental companies could invite the stations to put together a printout describing what they broadcast, to be given to customers. The tie-in opportunities using air space in airports, hotels, and rental cars boggle the mind.

The Air at Jiffy Lube

I am hooked on Jiffy Lube. I bought into its advertisement that if I take my car in for a check-up every 3,000 miles I will enhance its resale value. Further, the car will always have the right amounts of oil and air in the tires, and its filters, plugs, points, and fuses will be as good as new.

I trust Jiffy Lube. I do not trust the service departments at car dealerships. They have done nothing to earn my trust. They always gouge me, the car is never ready when they say it will be, and I feel like I am on enemy soil whenever I go there.

At Jiffy Lube—and its competitors—the bill is rarely over $50.00, the mechanics tell you what they did and ask your permission to do the higher-priced job before they do it, and you have a permanent record in the Jiffy Lube computer of all of your checkups so that you can document the tender loving care that you gave your car when you go to sell it.

But Jiffy Lube is missing an easy lay-up. While I am waiting the 30 minutes that it takes to service my car, I would be pleased to spend some money with these people, whom I like so much anyhow. Their waiting rooms have plenty of air space. I could be offered:

- Music cassettes
- Books on cassette
- Cup holders
- Key chains
- Flashlights
- Second key magnetic an-
  titheft devices

- Cards
- Floor mats
- Tissue holders
- Inside mirrors
- Home videos
- Promotional cups
- Driving maps

The space is free, and I am a captive in it. I am in a good (translates to "open to buy") mood because I am oiling the wheels on my chariot. I can be sold about $20 worth of product.

And why doesn't Jiffy Lube offer me the opportunity to read the "Jiffy Lube" magazine or join its users group or earn frequent-lube-job points giving me discounts on pizza dinners in a tie-in with the Pizza Hut next door? Plus, the demographics on Jiffy Lube customers must be fairly upscale—after all, we are worshipping at the First Church of Lubrication on a Saturday morning rather than crawling under the cars ourselves with an oil rag and an oil pan. Why not give us something to read about car insurance or travel? I might even watch a television show with travel tips paid for by one of the credit-card companies or an airline.

Downline Marketing

Once you free up the salesperson's time from prospecting through list rentals and from testing the lists, the salesperson is free for downline marketing. This strategy is sometimes referred to as networking, multilevel marketing, or even party-plan selling. To avoid confusion with any prior conceptions or misconceptions you might have, I call it downline marketing.

This system rewards salespersons for hiring and training salespersons responsible to them—hence, downline—as much as it does for their sales effort. It has been used effectively in insurance sales and by companies, such as Mary Kay Cosmetics and Tupperware, that sell at parties.

Downline marketing works best when the salesperson uses his or her home as an office and uses the customer's living room or kitchen as selling space. That is truly "free" space, paid for by the customers. Why do field sales offices exist? For prestige? As advertisements for the parent?

Most services can be sold by salespersons operating out of their homes and connected to the home or regional office by several umbilical cords—telephone, modem, and fax. (Soon we will add video conferencing and faxing from laptop computers to the list.)

Insurance and mutual funds are best sold in a downline modality where everyone is both *seller* and *trainer*. If you can sell, you can teach others to sell, but if you are better at teaching than at selling, you will still make lots of commission dollars—in overrides, rather than in straight commissions. Your ability to train others is enhanced by the availability of technology, such as videotapes, audiocassettes, modems, and fax machines. All of this was predicted in 1956 by Marshall McLuhan:

> Paradoxically electronic man shares much of the outlook of preliterate man because he lives in a world of simultaneous information, which is to say, a world of resonance in which all data influence other data.[1]

The Xerox machine made every person a publisher; the fax machine makes everyone a reader. It beckons us to remove the faxed message and read the obviously urgent message. If you need 30 prospects, you fax the home office, and the prospects' names are on your fax machine in the morning. If you need training materials for your three new hires, the materials are faxed to their machines, as well as yours. Videotapes can be overnighted. Printed mailings from other home offices can be modemed to your or your trainee's personal computer and pulled through your or her color laser printer in multiple copies, bound together, and put into the car for the next day's in-home marketing calls.

Fixed office sites are not needed in many businesses anymore. The portable cellular telephone—11 million were in use in mid-1992—obviates the need to be in an office or at home in order to receive or to make a telephone call. Fixed assets are increasingly irrelevant in marketing. Portable assets are the current wave, and they permit an efficient sales manager to hire and train dozens of people, judge their efforts quickly, retrain them, rejudge their performance, keep the good ones, and excess the weak ones.

A Downline System

Avoid thinking about your salespeople as individuals having jobs. Jobs imply boxes, with lines linking them to other boxes. Jobs imply edges and margins and grids. Electronic information removes barriers and grids. It minimizes the reliance on committees and regular meetings. Geometry gives way to abstract forms. Quantity, ownership of assets, plant, and equipment yield their importance in industry to flex-time, diversity, multiple specialties, and life brought back to human scale.

One of America's fastest growing and most valuable companies—Microsoft—could operate from any location with three people because its product—software—is intellectual. Its employees could sit in their homes in Taiwan, the Hebrides, Budapest, and Atlanta and send their work to a central place by satellite. The worker and the assigner of work are tied together by pattern recognition on their screens.

And so it is with sales forces. Most salespersons are good at selling or training. Some are good at both. Take away the job of prospecting, and give it to the microchip. Then you can build a low-maintenance sales force made up of salespeople and trainers, with the upline people earning commissions on the throughput of the downline people whom they hire. In this system, every downline person knows that he or she can equal or exceed the income of the person who hired him or her, and the person above that person, and so forth. The principle of the downline marketing strategy is that everyone gets a *fraction of the action* of the persons he or she hired and who are downline from him.

There are some rules. After all, downline marketing is a game, and games have winners and losers, as determined by the rules. The rules set forth each participant's commission at each level in the line, which is typically six persons deep. For instance, the first person in the line must sell $3,000 per month of product in year one and hire and train two new people per month who fill Level A in order to earn the highest level of commission available. The Level A person must sell $2,250 of product per month in her first year and hire and train two people, who fill Level B. The Level B person must sell $1,750 of product per month in her first year and hire and train 1.5 persons, who occupy Level C. And so forth.

The sales hurdles rise in the ensuing years, and replacement hires are needed to keep all of the slots filled. To keep the pot brewing, sales carry higher commissions if they develop into annuity sales in subsequent years. Sales that cancel shortly after the salesperson receives her commission carry steep penalties.

Who is leveraged in this system? The downline salespersons. They sell their family and friends in the first month or two, and, if those customers are satisfied, they begin to go outside their immediate circle and contact others. They then buy prospect lists from the parent, who captures them in the chip. If this sounds like a game, it is. Salespeople in the 1980s said, "I had an office, but I was never there." Salespeople in the 1990s say, "I don't have an office. Where I am is my office."

But sales achievements must be celebrated. The leader of the tribe calls everyone in every level to a watering hole four times a year to celebrate achievement. Trophies are awarded. There is great cheering and shouting and rejoicing. It may be the conference room at a Marriott, but with all the noise, it could be the locker room of the University of Tennessee after a win over the hated Alabama Crimson Tide.

I attended a Kentucky Fried Chicken franchisees' meeting in the early 1970s, when Colonel Sanders was still alive. Every franchisee wore a string tie, with a small sculpture in brass of the Colonel as the clasp. Franchisees who were new wore clasps with rubies (or red glass) in the Colonel's eyes. Senior franchisees wore clasps with diamonds in the eyes. The Colonel's clasp was made out of gold. Is this primitive? Maybe. I choose to call it celebrating a marketing system that works.

Note

1. George Sanderson and Frank MacDonald, *Marshall McLuhan: The Man and His Message* (Golden, Col.: Fulcrum, 1989), p. 71.

Stage Four
New Product Innovation

21

Predicting the Success of Your New Products

You are sitting on a pile of cash at this point, approximately 90 days into developing a gatekeeper management program. You have been a busy manager these last few months, slashing expenses, locating cash trapped in assets, spinning off divisions, and negotiating new prices with lawyers, accountants, ad agencies, health insurers, overnight couriers, suppliers of raw material, your sales force or rep organization, and just about anybody else who got in your way. Several new marketing channels have been opened and the newly found customers are responsive to your products, newsletters, bouncebacks, video news releases, and bouncy headlines.

But you haven't introduced a new product in over a year. You haven't upgraded a product in nearly two years. Your company is beginning to talk the talk but doesn't walk the walk. Sure, you have an efficient operation. Of course you are selling through multiple marketing channels. But your products have whiskers. They lack a freshness. They are last week's newspaper, herring wrappers. It is time to innovate some incredibly exciting new products.

Ensuring the Success of a New Product

To guarantee your innovation's success, have the manager perform the DEJ (demonstrable economic justification) factor test prior to innovating the new product or service. The manager asks: Does this opportunity meet eight all the requirements of the DEJ factor test? If it possesses all eight of the following factors, I can almost guarantee that *the manager can be virtually assured of success.* Plus, *the cost of entering the market will be less than $100,000.*

On the other hand, managers who fail to ask these eight questions may introduce a product or service into a new market and meet with failure. The DEJ factor test is a predictor of success and a measure of the cost of seizing the opportunity. Here's the rule:

- *Super DEJ:* If the new market possesses all eight DEJ factors, entering it will cost less than $100,000, and the probability of success will be about 90%.
- *Majority DEJ:* If the new market possesses seven out of eight DEJ factors, entering it will cost up to $1 million, and the probability of success will be about 80%.
- *Marginal DEJ:* If the new market possesses six out of eight DEJ factors, entering it will cost up to $20 million, and the probability of success will be about 60%.
- *Fewer than six DEJ factors:* The new market will reject the product or service at a cost of more than $20 million.

As you review the eight DEJ factors, think of a marketing failure within your company. Which two or more DEJ factors nailed its coffin shut? If you can't come up with an example inside your company, remember the DeLorean Motor Company, a $165 million fatal plunge.

The DEJ Factor Test

DEJ Factor	Ask	The Cost
1. Existence of qualified buyers	Are the consumers to whom this product or service is marketed *aware* that they have a need for it?	Advertising
2. Large number of buyers	Are there lots of consumers who need this product or service?	Competitive pressure on price
3. Homogeneity of buyers	Will the market accept a standardized product or service, or must it be customized?	Manufacturing, tooling, die costs

DEJ Factor	Ask	The Cost
4. Existence of competent sellers	Is the product or service so complex to explain that customers will need 90 days or more to test it?	Salespersons' salaries and expenses
5. Lack of institutional barriers to entry	Is there a requirement for governmental or industry association approval before the product or service can be marketed?	Working capital that burns while approval is awaited
6. Easy promotability by word-of-mouth	Can the product's or service's merits be described by consumers by word-of-mouth?	Advertising
7. Invisibility of the inside of the company	Is there a need to reveal profit margins to the public?	Competitive pressure on price
8. Optimum price/cost relationship	Is the selling price at least five times the cost of goods sold?	Restricts the number of marketing channels

Hold the DEJ factor test up to the DeLorean Motor Company and you will see why that company had failure written all over it before it began.

DEJ Factors	The DeLorean Car
1. Existence of qualified buyers	Consumers of cars have most of their needs filled by existing models. Strike this one. Seven to go.
2. Large number of buyers	There are many consumers who will buy novelty items. Still seven to go.
3. Homogeneity of buyers	No customizing. Still seven to go.

DEJ Factors	The DeLorean Car
4. Existence of competent sellers	Need to create a dealership, but that can be done by franchising. Still seven to go.
5. Lack of institutional barriers to entry	Government regulations virtually blanket the automobile industry. Take off one DEJ Factor. Six factors to go.
6. Easy promotability by word-of-mouth	An absence of competitive advantages did not provide many features to promote. Strike a third DEJ Factor. Five factors to go.
7. Invisibility of the inside of the company	The financing problems of the company were followed as closely as Princess Di's shopping trips to Sloane Street. Knock off the fifth DEJ Factor. Four factors to go.
8. Optimum price/cost relationship	The markup above cost of goods sold was in the neighborhood of three times, too small for marketing and promotion. Subtract another DEJ Factor. Three left and it's all over.

With only three DEJ factors, the DeLorean car was destined for disaster. It addressed a large market, it was standard rather than custom built, and it did not require a technically trained sales organization. Those three DEJ factors were insufficient to assure its viability.

22

Accelerating the Innovation Process

There are only three certainties in life: (1) death, (2) taxes, and (3) if a business doesn't change with the times, it will die. What are "the times"? They are the market's changing needs, its ebbs and flows. A company must continually innovate to meet those needs. I believe the innovation challenge is best met outside, by small, entrepreneurial think tanks. And there are plenty of data to support my contention that entrepreneurial companies bring new products to market better, faster, and cheaper than can established companies.

The prevailing view in the pharmaceutical industry is that the bigger a drug company, the greater its chances of success. During the late 1980s the industry was swept by a wave of mergers. With the cost of researching and developing new drugs soaring, possessing the biggest R&D budget and a huge marketing team to sell new drugs worldwide seemed the best way to succeed. No one in the industry was surprised that, by 1990, America's Merck and Britain's Glaxo, the industry's two most profitable companies, were also its two biggest.

Yet, in a study of the industry, David Matheson and Craig Wheeler, consultants with the Boston Consulting Group (BCG), challenge the "bigger is better" view.[1] In the steel and shipbuilding industries, where scale is important, a cluster of corporations dominate. But Merck and Glaxo, though the drug industry's biggest and most successful companies, each hold a mere 5 to 6 percent of the market. There are 14 other companies that have at least half that level of sales.

The dazzling success of Merck and Glaxo over the past decade, argue BCG's consultants, has less to do with size than with ability to combine capabilities, such as research, clinical trials, and marketing, which many of their rivals left compartmentalized. As a result, marketing managers at both companies talked to researchers to direct them toward the most common illnesses for which a profitable product could be designed. Developers talked to marketing people and researchers to determine which treatments regulators were likely to approve speedily. And researchers briefed both developers and marketing staff on technological possibilities. "It was in this cross-functional blending that Merck and Glaxo shone," says Matheson.[2]

By fusing distinct skills, the two companies created more efficient engines for getting products to market. Merck's forte was its ability to identify promising categories of drugs early. Glaxo had speed, rapidly bringing to market a few important drugs in many countries at once.

Neither Merck nor Glaxo expanded their research budgets in the 1980s. So how did they develop more new products faster than did other pharmaceutical companies? The answer: They invested in entrepreneurial companies.

Strategic Alliances

Typical of Glaxo's strategic alliances is its deal with Amylin Pharmaceuticals. The two companies entered into a strategic alliance in October 1991 to develop and commercialize Amylin's blockade therapy, which is intended to block the production, secretion, or action of a pancreatic hormone, as a treatment for adult-onset diabetes. Glaxo agreed to loan Amylin $2 million, to pay it $1 million plus future royalty payments, and to commit up to 35 scientists. It also agreed to invest approximately $200,000 in Amylin's common stock.

Merck entered into strategic alliances with, among others, Immulogic Pharmaceutical Corporation, a biopharmaceutical company that develops products to treat allergies and autoimmune diseases. In return for exclusive rights to commercialize certain products for the prevention or treatment of diabetes, rheumatoid arthritis, and organ transplant rejection, Merck is funding a research program at Immulogic and has invested $10.3 million in Immulogic through purchases of equity and $6.1 million in funding.

Merck, Glaxo, and other pharmaceutical giants know that to try to bring new products to market from within their organizations is futile. There are far too many tollgates within their companies that block new ideas unless they are recognized and credited. To get around the tollgates, these companies have allied themselves with outside consultants or outside entrepreneurial companies.

The same applies to you in your $5 million manufacturing or service company or your $20 million distribution company. The best ideas are likely to come from outside your company. To develop and bring them to market, you should seriously consider a strategic alliance with an entrepreneurial company.

Try Cooperation

The essence of business, as I have said, is to make your product or service a substitute for all other products or services and to make other products or services no substitute for yours.

If you cannot develop your product or service, if you cannot produce your product or service, or if you cannot get it into the marketplace, then you cannot tell whether or not it will be a substitute for all others. Therefore, you must cooperate with partners who can help you meet these milestones.

There are certain times when you should cooperate, rather than compete, with perceived competitors. There are more potential partners in your industry than you probably ever conceived of, once you begin assigning the title "potential strategic ally" to companies that used to fall under the heading "perceived competitor." You can materially reduce the costs of developing, producing, testing, building a sales force, and getting a product into the marketplace by cooperating with an entrepreneurial company, rather than attempting to develop, innovate, and bring new products to market on your own.

Using Strategic Alliances to Save R&D Dollars

Imagine yourself walking into the department at your company—enginering or marketing—that is responsible for new product development and saying the following:

"You, ladies and gentlemen, must invest your own money, or raise it outside this organization, in order to bring your new product ideas to a prototype stage. Borrow money if you like. Take out second mortgages on your homes. Ask your spouses to work two jobs. Obtain government grants and SBA loans. We will not put you on salary or pay any expenses until you have a working prototype that we can see.

"Then, before we invest money to produce the product and market it for you, we reserve the right to have the production and marketing departments analyze the device. That shouldn't take more than four to six months. Finally, depending on the whims of our finance committee, which meets twice a year, and depending on the state of the economy, not to mention the stock market and other commitments for our capital, we may or may not make an investment in your new product. That's our deal. Take it or leave it."

The effect, of course, would be the wholesale resignation of most of the personnel in the R&D department. Yet this scenario is in fact exactly what the entrepreneurial process is all about. Entrepreneurs shoulder the bulk of the risk for product development. The large corporations obtain leverage on their early efforts by investing in the companies *after* the early-stage risks are taken. Accordingly, the large corporations can reduce their investment in R&D by investing in entrepreneurial companies *after* the products have been developed and tested.

Incubating and Reducing the Cost of Acquisitions

Many companies troll for innovation in entrepreneurial ponds with an option to acquire a larger percentage ownership of the companies they invest in at some point in the future, subject to a number of factors, including performance, at a predetermined date and at a predetermined multiple of earnings. The purpose of investing with the option to acquire is to provide the strategic partner with lower-cost acquisitions. In addition, the company's close working relationship with members of the large corporation's management will have provided the corporation with a better knowledge of the company it is acquiring, thereby reducing the chance of buying a pig in a poke.

Philips Electronics, N.V., a Dutch consumer electronics giant, controls the 600-outlet video-store chain Super Clubs. It recently exercised $66 million of options to become the largest outside investor in the video retail giant Blockbuster Entertainment. Philips manufactures a significant number of videocassettes and audiocassettes. The potential for synergy is obvious. Monsanto Company, which derives approximately 40% of its $4.5 billion in revenues from fertilizer sales, has made several investments in agricultural genetics companies, with the intent of acquiring the first one that proves its ability to eliminate farmers' need for fertilizer by nitrogen fixation of the soil.

Since not all investments of the venture capital subsidiary will result in ownership of profitable companies, it may take a number of investments to create desirable acquisitions. However, if the strategic partner's overall loss ratio can be held to a reasonable level, incubating acquisitions through the venture capital operation can be an efficient adjunct to an overall corporate growth plan.

Adding New Products to Existing Distribution Channels

Entrepreneurs bring products to market in one-fifth the time it takes large corporations. But you and established corporations like yours have established distribution channels to move products from the factory to the end users, and entrepreneurial companies desperately need access to consumers.

In a strategic partnering relationship where the entrepreneur needs marketing channels and the established corporation needs innovative products, the basis of the deal is a licensing arrangement.

When a large corporation chooses to license a small company's product, the entrepreneurial company is paid an advance and sells the right to market the product in certain regions or to certain industries. However, there is more. The entrepreneurial company usually persuades the strategic partner to make an investment in the entrepreneurial company's equity in order to make sure that the latter is sufficiently well-capitalized to allow it to develop product upgrades and to service end users.

A sample licensing agreement appears in Exhibit 22-1.

Exhibit 22-1. Sample licensing agreement.

THIS AGREEMENT is made between ENTREPRENEURIAL IDEAS, INC. (the "Company"), a Delaware corporation, whose business address is _____ , and DASHBOARD MANUFACTURING CORP. (the "Sponsor"), a corporation, whose address is _____.

WITNESSETH:

WHEREAS: The Company has pioneered the development of an alcohol-on-the-breath analyzer for automobile dashboards, as well as related technologies to mitigate DWI-related deaths and accidents; and

WHEREAS: The Company owns the exclusive rights to the product named the DWI-MITIGATOR, and

WHEREAS: The Sponsor produces automobile dashboards sold to auto-mobile manufacturers in U.S. plants; and

WHEREAS: Sponsor has examined the DWI-MITIGATOR device and is agreeable to implant it on a test basis in 100,000 of its 1994 model L1001 dashboards.

(continues)

Exhibit 22-1. (*continued*)

NOW THEREFORE:

1. Sponsor shall make itself available for up to 80 hours per month in the 12-month period commencing with the signing of this Agreement, and for each of the following years of this Agreement so long as the minimum royalties are paid by Company to Sponsor, for the purpose of preparing advertisements, endorsements, testimonials, public relations, and commercials on behalf of the Company and its DWI-MITIGATOR (the "Product").

2. Sponsor's image and name may be used on the packaging of the Product and on the printed matter that accompanies the Product, but Sponsor shall have the right to edit such packaging and printed matter. Sponsor shall return all edited materials to the Company within 15 days, or failing to do so, the Company will assume that Sponsor has approved it.

3. Sponsor shall have the right to approve any and all advertisements, endorsements, testimonials, and commercials for the Product.

4. Sponsor shall not unreasonably delay its review of editorial material sent to Sponsor by the Company and shall cooperate to the best of its ability toward the mutual objective of generating sales for the Product.

5. In consideration therefore, Sponsor agrees to pay Company a royalty of two and one-half percent (2.5%) of the gross selling price of the Product by Sponsor North America for five (5) years from the date of this Agreement, such payment to be made on June 30 and December 31 of each year.

6. This Agreement shall be terminable by Company in the event that Company does not receive minimum royalties from Sponsor of one million dollars ($1 million) per annum; said accounting period shall begin nine (9) months after the first test sales of the Product and its attachments in their final design. The Sponsor anticipates raising more than $2,000,000 to launch the product, and in its business plan the Sponsor projects fifth-year sales of 500,000 units at a retail selling price of $89.95.

7. Sponsor shall pay Company an advance against such royalty payment of fifty thousand ($50,000) dollars upon the signing of this Agreement, and the advance shall be deducted from the first royalty payment.

8. The gross selling price shall be defined as the gross sales receipts paid to the Company by customers, less returns, unpaid taxes, shipping and handling charges, and customer's duties, if any.

9. Sponsor shall summarize all sales data in dollars and units on a monthly basis and deliver it to Company within 20 days after the last day of each month at the above address.

10. Sponsor shall be given fifty (50) models of the Product, without charge, for its professional use.

11. Sponsor may not endorse a competitive product unless the Company ceases operations.

12. Company may request an examination of the Sponsor's books and records having to do with the Product, to be conducted by qualified representatives skilled in accounting. The examination shall take place following two weeks' written notice at the Sponsor's principal place of business, during usual business hours, at Company's expense.

13. This Agreement shall constitute the entire agreement between the Parties and shall be construed under the laws of the State of _____.

ENTREPRENEURIAL IDEAS, INC.

by: _____

_____

_____

_____
Date

DASHBOARD MANUFACTURING CORP.

by: _____

_____

_____

_____
Date

Notes

1. "The Big Pill," *The Economist* (March 6, 1993), p. 60.
2. Ibid.

23

Acquiring Gatekeeper Companies

Has the thought occurred to you to acquire another company or several other companies this year? Perhaps not. Perhaps you have not had the cash to think on a broad scale. Or, perhaps, the purpose of an acquisition has not come into sharp focus.

There is a good reason to consider an acquisition: to achieve a corporate makeover as a tollgate operator. The means to finance the acquisition come from employing leveraged buyout (LBO) financing techniques. Most LBOs have been achieved by entrepreneurial companies that had very little cash. Moreover, many of the most successful LBOs involved the takeover of companies that collect their cash up front and use the customers' money as capital. Conversely, many of the most disastrous LBOs have been takeovers of capital equipment manufacturers that are unable to service debt in cyclical downturns because they are waiting for customers to pay them.

A corporate makeover that changes the mix of revenues in your company so that you receive cash up front, rather than being paid last, and that changes the strategy by which you run your company to always being paid from always paying out is the goal of gatekeeper management.

Acquiring Tollgate Companies

Look at Warren Buffett, Henry Singleton, Saul Steinberg, Rupert Murdoch, Laurence Tisch, Henry Kravis, and other takeover entrepreneurs. They began with simple ideas, collected data, assimilated it, persuaded others to believe in their plan, then bought companies that fulfilled their dreams, using leveraged buyout financing techniques. These gatekeeper deities do not buy smokestack America;

they buy *tollgates*. Buffett, Singleton, Steinberg, and Tisch began their careers in the acquisition business by acquiring insurance companies. Murdoch began by buying newspapers and magazines, Kravis, by buying supermarket chains and other retailers. These kinds of companies have the inherent leverage that is necessary to extract tolls from others—many others.

Tollgate companies—retailers, financial service providers, distributors—differ from *products* companies in that they control access to highways of consumers. Thus, gatekeeper companies have inherent leverage, which they use to inversely leverage products companies that seek to have the gatekeeper companies carry their products. A products company produces and delivers a product, ships it to a gatekeeper company, and waits to be paid as the gatekeeper company resells it to a consumer. A gatekeeper company is paid by consumers in advance or at the point of sale and delivers its products in the future, if on a subscription basis, or at the point of sale. That is *inherent* leverage. It makes gatekeeper companies many times more liquid than products companies.

Gatekeeper companies have the ability to generate far more sources of cash flow than do products companies. Take the typical newspaper. It generates cash flow four ways, without even taking into account innovative ways to repackage and market information:

- Advertisements
- Subscriptions
- Newsstand sales
- List rentals

When a newspaper is taken over by a gatekeeper manager, whether from outside or inside, and begins introducing changes, the newspaper multiplies its sources of cash flow. This is *profound* leverage, which is easier to achieve in gatekeeper companies than in capital- or inventory-intensive companies. Here are some of the additional cash-flow sources that managers of newspapers or magazines can implement:

- Resale of news stories to other publishers
- Repackaging of stories as videotapes
- Repackaging of stories as audiocassettes
- Running of seminars led by highly regarded columnists
- Capturing of critical information on electronic media to be resold as a "news utility" (Reuters and the Telerate subsidiary of *The Wall Street Journal*)

- Sale of books comprising special-interest articles (e.g., *The New York Times Cookbook*)
- Sale of articles on topical issues such as health care, diet, and gardening to small-town newspapers to be used as "Sunday Features"
- Creation of joint ventures with direct mail companies wishing to sell products via mail order to the magazine's or newspaper's readers
- Acquisition of television and radio stations to spread the cost of gathering news stories
- Gathering of specialized articles for target marketing (e.g., health care articles in magazine form for resale to physicians for their waiting rooms)
- Sale of special-interest articles to selected customers via a newsletter
- Sale of publications in foreign languages
- Sale of premium and gift items (e.g., tote bags, T-shirts, book-ends, birthdate publications)
- Spin-off of sister publications

Not all magazine and newspaper publishers are generating cash flow from the 18 different sources just listed. If you can spot one or two that have fallen short of the mark and acquire them inexpensively, you could do a makeover of your products company within a year.

Sample Tollgate Companies

Retail Chains

Why own a retail chain? Because you can charge others tolls to gain access to your customers. Here are some of the channels that a retailer can tack onto its basic business of selling groceries, hardware, pharmaceuticals, or lumber:

- Creation of frequent-purchasers club that offers awards, premiums, and bonuses
- Rental of advertising space on shopping carts and shopping bags and on the sides of soft-drink machines
- Rental of aisle space for point-of-sale promotions
- Rental of air space at checkout counters to capture information

- Joint ventures with vendors who pay the retailer to provide in-store services
- Collection of slotting allowances (tolls paid by vendors to test new products on valuable shelf space)
- Rental of front-of-store space for recycling programs
- Installation of end-of-aisle buckets for vendors who want their products to be sold at a high volume
- Installation of J-hooks (jut-out-of-the-aisle promotional space)
- Sale or rental of information about products
- Collection of data on product sales for sale to vendors and others
- Development of Seal of Approval marketing

Drive through any town of 10,000 or more inhabitants in the United States and you will see that the most drastic physical changes in recent years have occurred among retailers. There are relatively few retail survivors from 30 years ago; like the musical chairs game, swifter and more agile retailers have replaced the old guard. The new stores that you see have been either started by entrepreneurial companies or taken over and redirected by corporate raiders ("financial entrepreneurs"). Wal-Mart has reshaped the landscape most significantly, but you can't ignore Safeway, Stein-Mart, Office Depot, Home Depot, Price Club, Costco, and the smaller but ubiquitous retailers of specialty products and services, such as McDonald's, Blockbuster Video, The Foot Locker, Little Caesar's, Computerland, The Gap, and B. Dalton.

The retailers that have gone by the wayside were taking up space, not making new commercial statements. Business is like the ocean. Sharks are the great predator survivors. Sharks either keep swimming forward or die. In the 1990s, when there is an excess of vacant retail space, creative entrepreneurs are continually introducing new products and services that consolidate and cut down to size some of the more overblown and costly ideas of the 1980s.

Insurance Companies

The primary objective of the raiders who have acquired insurance companies is to have and to control captive sources of capital. The objectives of entrepreneurs who have launched insurance companies is to seize opportunities and capture niche markets that the giant, existing insurers have overlooked.

You can start an insurance company today if you have identified a risk that you would like to "buy" and that you can persuade reinsurers to backstop. However, it takes a long time to reach positive cash flow. Consequently, acquiring an existing insurance company with a historic book of business, state licenses, assets, cash flow, and trained people and then adding your strokes to this canvas is the preferred route. Such companies are some of the *best* gatekeepers because of the myriad inherent leveraging opportunities:

- Agents are assigned territories and trained by the company, but they work for commission only and do not receive draws or expense reimbursements.
- Agents pay an up-front fee to purchase their training materials.
- Most insurance companies set their premiums at 200% or more of their expected loss payouts and reinsure (i.e., trade out a substantial part of the losses in exchange for part of the premiums) against catastrophic claims, so they build up cash.
- Insurance companies invest their cash in bonds and stocks, and some make venture capital investments, which occasionally generate unusually high returns.
- Insurance companies enjoy excellent downline marketing opportunities by which agents are compensated with overrides for signing other agents. If done correctly, this process multiplies cash flow.
- Insurance companies have the opportunity for affinity marketing through associations that lead to multichannel marketing opportunities modeled on the users group format.
- Insurance companies can profit from fronting fees (fees received for "loaning" their state licenses to unlicensed insurance agency organizations that lack underwriting capability). The fees can be as high as 20% of premiums.
- Some insurers reinsure the policies of other insurers for additional fee income; the insured risk is then partially reinsured with another carrier.
- Insurance companies can form joint ventures with noncompetitive insurers to market one another's products.

Evaluating Your Own Marketing Approach

Ask yourself if you are marketing your company's products through as many channels as are these gatekeeper companies. The answer will most likely come back "No." Then ask yourself if you would like to have cash flowing into your company from 12 to 18 channels, most of which do not require a capital investment to build. The answer will most likely come back "Yes."

Then visualize either developing (that costs money) or buying (that requires borrowing money) a gatekeeper company. Saul Steinberg, the corporate raider, buys gatekeeper companies, repays his lenders by selling off assets, then sells the fully leveraged company to the public or to others. Steinberg acquired Reliance Insurance Company in the 1970s using the stock of Leasco, his computer leasing company. His Days Inn "flip" is one of the classics of fast capital gains by any raider standards.

In 1984 Steinberg acquired Days Inn of America, an economy motel chain, for $275 million through his insurance-based holding company, Reliance Capital Group. Reliance then spent 18 months converting the company-owned motels to franchises, generating $420 million in cash as they were sold to their operators. Steinberg paid down his debt, kept the company, and netted approximately $145 million.

Plan Your Attack

If you produce or distribute a product or service sold through retailers, it is both interesting and worthwhile to hypothesize your takeover of a supermarket, hotel, or drugstore chain. Then see how many of the newspaper or insurance industry cash-flow multiplying channels you can implement in your retail chain. The mind boggles at the cash-flow leveraging ability of channel companies.

You simply cannot generate that many cash-flow channels with a products or service company. This is important if you own a capital equipment manufacturer with a mountain of debt and are searching for ways to generate additional cash flow. Before you buy the neighborhood restaurant or supermarket, remember that LBOs are a world unto themselves, with their own rules and fundamentals.

Using a Defensive Strategy

The acquisition business is defensive in nature. The winners are those who keep their heads under the hood. The losers are those who prance around the track shouting, "Look what I bought. Look what I own." Ownership can be yours for a fleeting moment. If you cannot service the acquisition debt, you will regret for years to come your brief moment in the limelight.

The best defensive strategy is to discover the multiple ways to increase cash flow post-acquisition without spending cash. Sure, it is easier when you acquire a channel company. But there are additional sources of cash flow waiting for you in products companies, as well. First, I describe some channels that exist in *consumer* products companies; then I move on to *industrial* products companies.

Consumer Products Companies

The key to developing multiple sources of cash flow if your company manufactures consumer products is to *think channel*. You want to capture the names, addresses, and any other information you can gather about your customers. Their sex, age, and years of education would be wonderful information to have. With that information, you learn who your customers are and why they buy your product, and you can begin to create channels to them for the sale of other products and services. I once invested in a 50-year-old company with $5 million in annual sales and a $250,000 of cash flow at a valuation of $1 million. It sold 3 million products per year to supermarkets, drugstores, convenience stores, and catalog companies, all in cellophane bags, but it had never collected a single customer name (except for the names on the approximately 3,500 letters from customers it received and responded to each year but did not otherwise use). The types of innovative marketing strategies that I introduced were simple but effective. They included:

* *The Bounceback*. To capture customer information, we put into each bag a small piece of paper announcing a game with a trip to Hawaii as the prize. Over 150,000 names were collected in six months.
* *Rentals of Customer Lists*. We rented the customer list through list brokers to magazines, catalog companies, and other consumer products manufacturers that want to reach this generic group of consumers. We generated $100,000 in free cash flow in 12 months.
* *Marketing of Information*. We published a newsletter of useful information related to the products, using suggestions in the 3,500 customer letters to describe myriad uses of the company's products. We sold the back page of the newsletter to an advertiser. By doing this, we generated $24,000 in free cash flow.
* *Product Judging*. We began a product review group through which, for a fee, 1,000 customers (selected from the letters and 150,000 game players) were given the privilege of judging the company's new products before they come onto the market and of buying the products at a 30% discount off retail price. The product reviews

people paid the company $500 apiece for the privilege, producing $50,000 in free cash flow.

• *Catalog Business.* We launched a catalog, and charge advertising space to innovative gift and novelty manufacturers for appearing in the catalog (*The Sharper Image* strategy). We raised $225,000 in cash flow, which paid for the catalog launch.

The bottom line is that we invested $20,000 in developing five new channels that in turn generated $374,000 in free cash flow. The catalog launch was fully funded by product advertisers and generated $600,000 in first-year sales at a profit of $240,000 before interest and debt service. By thinking channel, the company ended its first-year post-acquisition period with $396,000 in cash flow after interest and debt service, two-thirds more than pre-acquisition cash flow.

There are other cash-flow generating strategies that the consumer products company can introduce, all of them information-based and all of them paid for by a third party. I guarantee you that your sales can triple if you think channel and begin to gather information about your customers. Moreover, if you find a consumer products manufacturer to acquire that is not collecting information about its customers and if you acquire it cheaply enough, you have just put your youngsters into the Association of Trust Fund Children.

Capital Equipment Manufacturers

The ability to generate multiple sources of cash flow in companies that manufacture and sell their products to other companies is difficult but not impossible if you "key off" the watchword of our age: *information*. Let's assume that the target company manufactures computers, industrial controls, metal-stamping presses, or machinery. You buy the company, we'll say, with maximum leverage and no disposable cash flow with which to expand. Many capital equipment LBOs fail because the takeover entrepreneurs think that they have only two options: to sell more product to existing customers or to hire more salesmen (or buy more advertising) to reach new customers. That is a false assumption. The truth lies with information.

Let me show you what some gatekeeper managers are doing to enhance cash flow in their capital equipment companies.

• *Form users groups.* To reiterate, these are customer clubs formed by vendors to provide a forum for the exchange of ideas among users of the vendors' products. The users are charged an annual fee, typically ranging from $1,000 to $5,000, which is used to enhance the vendors' products or to make more radical innovations along the lines recommended at the annual users group meeting.

• *Sell new product at seminars.* The purpose of the users group meeting or seminar, which is paid for by the users as well, is to create personal contact between the users and the vendor. New products or services are introduced, accounts receivables collected, and serious customer schmoozing is done up and down the corridors of the hotel. Cassettes and books of the seminar are sold to nonattendeees.

• *Use expo, or air space, marketing.* Some manufacturers invite producers of peripheral products to attend their users group meetings and to exhibit their products in small booths for a fee. Known as *expo* marketing, this strategy has been used by companies such as Hewlett-Packard and Apple Computer for years to generate additional cash flow. Twenty-five exhibitors, each paying $500 four times a year, contribute $500,000 of gross-equals-net cash flow, and the company enjoys profound leverage because the space it is renting is air space; the users group is paying for the meeting, so the company is "selling" the same space twice, and the exhibitors are paying the vendor for the privilege of meeting the vendor's customers.

• *Keep quoting until they blink.* Another way to increase cash flow is to keep quoting services and add-ons until the customer blinks his or her eyes. The company may be selling a capital goods product to industrial customers that also need advice on installation, tips on usage, and information on provisions for servicing. Therefore, it may be possible to generate additional cash flow from each product sale by charging for freight, installation, user training, service and maintenance, a repair warranty, and a 900 hotline (for which the caller pays). These add-ons can be imbedded in a fully marked-up price and pulled away, with small reductions in price, if the buyer does not want some of them.

A word about service add-ons in service businesses. You can dramatically improve your cash flow if you perform your services at the client's site and add on other jobs while your crew is there. Pentokil, one of the United Kingdom's most successful publicly held service companies, used to be exclusively a pest-control service company. When Clive Thompson took over the reins in 1982, he developed a range of environmental services, including providing and caring for tropical plants, disposing of medical waste, and cleaning offices, shops, and kitchens. Earnings grew 21% a year from

1982, reaching $192 million in 1992 on sales of $580 million. Customers rarely haggle price in the service areas that Pentokil has chosen to operate.

Looking for Cash-Flow Opportunities

You may miss out on some excellent acquisition candidates if you fail to observe the cash-flow opportunities that the target company's current owners are ignoring. Sellers unload companies for many reasons, but in the main these companies do not generate a sufficiently large return above cost. Or, stated as the inverse, the sellers believe that they cannot work much harder or get their capital to work much harder to generate significantly greater returns than they are already doing.

But that is the logic of another age. Today, working hard is less relevant than working smart. Moving matter is less relevant than gathering, analyzing, and utilizing information.

This thought leads me to Silver's Law of Gatekeeping:

Any company's cash flow
can be increased by substituting
information for capital.

There is no company operating in the free market whose cash flow cannot be significantly increased by the innovative use of information without spending additional capital.

Once you understand this axiom and really begin to look at the money that most companies leave on the table in the course of customer contact, then you will begin to understand why the acquisition of gatekeeper companies is a trend that continues to grow and produce undreamed-of wealth for the acquirers. Gatekeeper managers understand the cash-flow generating power of information, whereas the targets operate as if we were still in an earlier decade, when ownership of hard assets and the means of production counted for something. The corporate raider Saul Steinberg, for example, looks at assets as objects that can be converted to cash. His favorite takeover targets seem to be retail chains, such as Days Inn, which he can acquire with leverage, then sell the company-owned sites to their managers, who then become franchisees. This allows him to recover his initial investment, repay his borrowers, and then sell the chain, fully franchised, to another buyer for a fabulous capital gain.

Practice Cash-Flow Sensing

To get a feel for how companies handle money, order the annual reports and brokerage house research reports for ten publicly held companies in different industries but of a size that you would be interested in acquiring. Review their financial statements in detail. Then list on a legal pad sources of cash flow that the ten companies have implemented. Compare the list to the nine additional sources of near-term cash flow listed here:

Consumer Product Manufacturer:

1. Capture customer names with a game.
2. Rent customer (and noncustomer) names to others.
3. Publish a free newsletter for customers; sell ad space.
4. Begin a product review group.
5. Initiate a private-label catalog.

Capital Equipment Manufacturer:

1. Form users groups.
2. Utilize seminar selling.
3. Rent expo space at seminars.
4. Charge for multiple services at point of sale.

Chances are you will find five or more cash-flow channels that the companies' managements have not begun to penetrate because they are so content with selling boxes of something and receiving payment 30 to 60 days in the future. If you ignore the cash-flow generating opportunities that the takeover candidates present, you will be seeing only half of the fascinating picture of the acquisition business.

Just Ask

Once you have analyzed the list of acquisition candidates and their possible cash-flow generating abilities, the next step is to visit the target companies and ask all of the relevant questions. This is the due diligence stage of an acquisition, and it is critical. Failure to ask the right questions could lead to the acquired company's going belly-up, with the lenders auctioning off the company's assets.

To assist you in your due diligence, Exhibit 23-1 lists all the questions you should ask when investigating an acquisition candidate.

Exhibit 23-1. Due diligence questions.

General Information

- Description of how the company sells its products
- Product/service distribution plans and sales forecast
- States in which corporation is qualified to do business
- Resumes of all senior officers of the company
- Organizational chart
- List of all officers and directors: name, title, salary for previous year, director's fees, current salary, and amount of stock held
- Copies of all employment contracts and bonus plans affecting compensation
- List of all affiliations
- List of principal shareholders, the amount and value of each stockholder's holdings, and other types of equity securities in the company
- List of any current or pending legal problems or lawsuits

Employees and Compensation Information

- List of all employees, including position, duties, and salary
- Total list of employees by number, department, and class; average number employed over last five years
- List of all independent contractors by name, title, and duties
- Corporate policies regarding sick pay, emergency leave, overtime, and regular working hours
- Information regarding any and all union activity
- Copy of the company's health insurance plan

Asset Information

- Address and description of all plants and offices owned or leased
- Copies of all leases
- Copies of all purchase contracts, if owned, title papers, appraisal, survey, and taxes currently paid on property
- Description and age of machinery and equipment, all office equipment and furniture, whether leased or owned, and serial numbers, date purchased, and price paid
- Lists of all other assets, inventories, accounts receivables, and bank accounts, including average balances
- Most recent accounts receivable aging

Trademark, Patent, and Copyright Information

- List of all trademarks, registration numbers, and dates of registration

(continues)

Exhibit 23-1. (*continued*)

- List of all patents, with patent numbers and dates
- List of all copyrights, with copyright numbers and dates
- Copies of all royalty and other agreements relating to patents and trademarks
- List of all patents, trademarks, and copyrights pending

Contracts and Commitments

- List and details of all contracts and commitments that may bind the company in any way
- Copies of signed letters of intent, agreements, and contracts

Financial Information

- Profit-and-loss statements and balance sheets of the corporation and all subsidiaries for the current year and for the past three years
- Copies of credit reports on corporation within last five years
- Copies of all tax returns for last five years
- Copies of all insurance policies
- List and details of other indebtedness and liabilities
- Copy of most recent accounts payable aging

Product/Service Information

- List of all products and current dollar sales volume and profit margins on each product
- Credit reports and/or annual reports on competitors
- Unit cost for each product and possible future cost increases
- Inventory list of important raw materials and packaging supplies as of last fiscal year
- Corporate break-even point and details of product mix and fixed and variable expenses
- List of commitments to purchase materials, long- and short-term
- List of major suppliers and names of backup suppliers
- Copies of service and/or product warranties
- Name of the most important trade journals read by the company

Selling Prices and Sales Outlets

- Price breakdown for each product, payment terms, other discounts, service, and returns
- List of sales outlets and complete information on each
- Sales statistics for past five years by significant categories
- List of major competitors

Advertising Information

- Name of advertising or public relations firm employed by the corporation and details of all TV and radio advertising
- Results of any surveys or market research studies done, formal and informal

Miscellaneous Information

- Newspaper and magazine articles about the company and its products or services
- Advertising brochures and manuals designed for client and consumer use
- Product samples
- Policy and procedural manuals

Pay Attention to Details

Do not rush the due diligence period. Ask all of the questions that you need to have answered. Then retire to your hotel room, get a good night's sleep, return to the company the next day, and ask some more. The company may be on the block because the owners wish to sell before the next cyclical downturn.

Notice small things, like the neatness of the company, the cleanliness of the factory floors, whether waste is stored in containers and sold, the morale of the employees, how early the parking lot fills up, the manner in which the telephone is answered, and the attitude of senior managers toward your questions. Look for problems; look for things that could go wrong. It is possible that the company has been prepared for a sale and that there is some window dressing put up on your behalf.

Lighten Up on the Ideology

If you keep boring in on the complex ideology of the prospective business relationship without interjecting some humor, the takeover candidate, auditing firm, lender, or other vendor may find your inquisitive style abrasive.

When you ask questions that affect the prospective business relationship, you are playing a business *game*. The object of a game is to win. Games end in the establishment of a winner and a loser. The more questions you ask, the more likely you will be the winner.

Successful venture capitalists will tell you that the losers have failed to ask questions before investing.

Watch out for myths. Myths and rituals, in the words of anthropologist and social philosopher Claude Levi-Strauss, "bring about a union between two initially separate groups,"[1] which stresses the collectivity of the faithful. When you receive a mythical answer such as "Our company has a 50-year-old reputation for quality products," the salesperson is attempting to reconstruct the business world by implying that "winners" use the salesperson's products, whereas losers choose those of a competitor.

To fall for a seller's myths and constructions is to wipe out the gains derived from probing for ways to save costs and to generate cash flow from the relationship. If you feel you must own a company that has a ritualistic, 50-year-old mythological background, then perhaps your self-esteem could benefit from some hydraulic support. Only weak buyers need to own 50-year-old companies whose economic validity is more a myth than a reality. Beware of mythical answers to your questions.

Kohlberg, Kravis, Roberts & Co. (KKR) has made 40 leveraged buyouts since 1976 at a cost of $65 billion, using less than $4 billion of its funds' capital. It is believed that only five of KKR's acquired companies are having difficulty servicing their debt. On the other hand, we read of other raiders who get into serious difficulty with one or two takeovers. How can one explain the difference between the winners and losers in the acquisition business? The answer is that the winners keep their heads under the hood searching for details. The losers speed around the track carrying a banner that reads, "Look at me. I made an acquisition."

Note

1. Claude Levi-Strauss, *The Savage Mind* (Chicago: University of Chicago Press, 1962), p. 32.

24

Forward Pricing

If you think that what you have been doing to rekindle your love affair with your company up to this point has been fun, I can only say this: "You ain't seen nothing yet." We're going to enter the big arena now, the main event—forward pricing.

Forward pricing is such an aggressive and tough business tactic that I have ascribed to it the Fundamental Law of Gatekeeping:

It's not over until I win.

Forward pricing was conceptually developed by little children being taught checkers or Go Fish by their parent. They lose ten straight games, and the parent says in exasperation, "Well, it's over. Let's get you to bed." To which the child responds, "No, Daddy. It's not over until I win." She wins the next game.

The Japanese brought the idea of forward pricing to the United States and knocked the American automobile and consumer electronics industries for a loop. Michael Milken, of the now-defunct firm of Drexel Burnham Lambert, used the concept with junk-bond takeovers and stood the investment banking industry on its ear. You can drive your competition to tears with forward pricing and capture over half the market.

To visualize forward pricing, think of a sliding board in a swimming pool. Try to remember yourself at age 5, sailing down the sliding board, laughing and shouting, and then the big splash when you hit the water. Fun like you've never had before, right? Yes. And you're about to do it again.

Where on the sliding board did you build up your greatest speed—at the top or at the bottom? Clearly, at the bottom. The same applies in production: The more production you push through the factory—yours or a subcontractor's—the lower the cost of goods sold and the less expensively you can price the product (see Exhibit 24-1).

If you know (and that's the key word) or have a great deal of

Exhibit 24-1. The sliding board of forward pricing.

$

The
Stuffee's
Pricing

Overhead

Manufacturing Cost

VOLUME

Forward Pricing: The initial price is set here and maintained throughout.

---

certainty that at 10,000 units per year your unit cost of goods sold will decline from $250 to $100, then you can drop your price *today*—at the top of the sliding board—from $400 per unit to $200 per unit. Sure, you will lose money as you go down the slide, but you will pick up customers from your competitors in droves.

The Genius of Soichiro Honda

No entrepreneur ever understood the principle of forward pricing better than this brilliant entrepreneur who captured significant chunks of the U.S. motorcycle and automobile markets. His premise was what I call *Silver's Rule of 30s:*

> You can produce a product that is 30% better, 30% more efficient, and 30% faster than its competitors, but to capture 30% of the market, it had better be 30% less expensive as well.

Honda knew that by entering new markets at prices 30% below the competition's, his products would sell like crazy. He also knew that production costs would drop as volume increased. Why wait two years to lower prices? Do it now and drive the competition crazy.

25

Checking Off the Gatekeeping List

The journey to multiply tenfold your company's cash flow in one year has ended. We have come a long way together, and with each step we have become more fearless and more understanding about our businesses. With our renewed enthusiasm we will be able to convert our employees to followers and to create teammates within our companies who champion our every move.

To paraphrase George Bernard Shaw: Successful people look about themselves to find the circumstances that they want, and if they can't find them they create them—and I would add, or acquire them. Will you make friends by putting up tollgates and charging fees? Probably not. But you will have more cash flow than will your critics. Money isn't everything, but it is important . . . up there with oxygen, perhaps.

Gatekeeping Is Personal Empowerment

The peculiar quality of greatness that we feel when we make over our companies, the sense of the sublimity of the occasion, stems from a delight in being alive and in control of events at a critical movement in the history of our industry, our community, our company. We thrive on change and the instability of things. The infinite possibilities of the unpredictable future offer endless opportunities for spontaneous moment-to-moment improvisation and for large, imaginative, bold strokes that bring about changes in the course of our industries. Our strength comes to us from our clear, brightly colored vision of— and passionate feeling for—our view of the future and our power to shape it. This strength—our love affair with our companies—enhances our energy and drives it.

Lest we forget the excitement of finding our identities in becoming gatekeepers, here is a checklist of the road we traveled together. Should you ever need a task while at work, turn to this page, select 1 of the 25 items on the list, and plunge into it with a gusto:

1. Talking to Your Landlord
   a. Rentable vs. usable space
   b. Common-area factors
2. Reexamining Your Communications Costs
   a. Postage savings (presorting, carrier route sorting)
   b. Overnight courier savings
   c. Telephone savings (least-cost routing, call accounting/cost accounting, codes toll restriction)
3. Slashing Health Care Insurance Costs
   a. Managed care
   b. Self-insurance
   c. Association-based health insurance
4. Rolling Back Legal Costs
   a. D&O insurance
   b. Refusing to train your law firm's associates
   c. Maintaining a talk sheet
   d. Going in-house
   e. Refusing to pay for bad legal opinions
   f. Keeping counsel honest
5. Are Your Advertising Costs Out of Line?
   a. Ads that answer consumer concerns
   b. Centripetal thinking
   c. Public relations
   d. Statement stuffers
   e. CEO testing
   f. The gift box
   g. Local public relations
   h. Duncan Hines wisdom
   i. Testimonial letters
   j. Video news releases
6. Renegotiating Your Loan Costs
   a. Reducing or eliminating origination, renewal, and cancellation fees
   b. Lowering interest rates
   c. Recourse vs. nonrecourse loans
   d. Benefits
   e. How to treat your banker

7. Cutting Your Accounting Costs
   a. Monitor the assignment of personnel.
   b. Know their hourly rates.
   c. Demand senior people; do not pay to train rookies.
   d. Insist on a management letter.
   e. Do as much work as possible inside.
   f. Will you defend your audit in court, if necessary, without charge to our company?
   g. Does your fee include a management letter?
   h. Who will be our partner-contact within your firm?
   i. Is your firm planning to remain in the community, or is there any chance that it may be moving out in the near future?
   j. Obtain an engagement letter.
8. Cutting Back Travel Costs
   a. Use of wholesale travel agents
   b. The 25% airline savings
   c. Rule 240
   d. Cuban missile crisis
   e. The Speedy Gonzalez ticket
9. Going Nose-to-Nose with Your Suppliers
   a. Just-in-time planning
   b. Customer-driven markets
   c. Flexible manufacturing
   d. Stretching your payables
10. Rethinking Your Employee Needs
    a. Employee leasing
11. Spinning Off Assets: Deciding What Is Core and What Is Peripheral
    a. Silver's First Law of the Core
12. Spinning Off Peripheral Divisions to Their Managers
    a. Holding onto a piece of the action
    b. Assessing an MBO
    c. Air ball financing
13. Facilities Management Spin-Offs
    a. Spinning off your entrepreneurial divisions
    b. Controlling the leverage in a divisional spin-off
    c. Itek
14. Sale-Leaseback of Hard Assets
    a. Sale-leaseback of office space
    b. Delivery vans and trucks
    c. Profiting on back-hauling

15. Renting Out Freed-Up Space
    a. Seeking tenants in related businesses
    b. Soft-dollar deals
    c. Van services
16. Finding Your Product's Demonstrable Economic Proposition
    a. The DEP factor ($V = P \times S \times M$)
    b. Multiple DEP factors
       (1) Service
       (2) Ancillary sales
       (3) Cooperation
       (4) List rentals
       (5) Insurance
       (6) Information sales
       (7) Back-door marketing
    c. The money-back guarantee
17. Multiplying Your Marketing Channels
    a. Monthly credit-card statements as shelf space
    b. The service add-on
    c. The users group
    d. Wall space marketing
    e. The Seal of Approval business
    f. Competing with yourself (before someone else does)
    g. Private labeling
18. Locating Noncustomers
    a. The information solution
    b. Progressive Corporation's information channel
    c. The jam producer's strategy
    d. Putting a microchip at the cash register
    e. Direct response marketing
    f. Artificial intelligence-based marketing
    g. Newsletters
19. Affinity Marketing
    a. Cooperating
    b. Developing tie-ins
20. Air Space ("Free") Marketing
    a. Free space inside the store
    b. Air space marketers
    c. Flea markets
    d. Car washes and other waiting rooms
    e. Barter
    f. Association-based marketing
    g. Downline marketing

Index